Integrating the Literature of Judy Blume in the Classroom

by
Thomas J. Palumbo

illustrated by Vanessa Filkins

Cover by Vanessa Filkins

Copyright © Good Apple, Inc., 1990

Good Apple, Inc.
1204 Buchanan St., Box 299
Carthage, IL 62321-0299

Other Books by Tom Palumbo

GA648 Tuesday Timely Teasers
GA649 Wednesday Midweek Winners
GA650 Thursday Think Time
GA1050 Language Arts Thinking Motivators
GA1095 Measurement Motivators

Copyright © Good Apple, Inc., 1990

ISBN No. 0-86653-558-6

Printing No. 987654321

Good Apple, Inc.
1204 Buchanan St., Box 299
Carthage, IL 62321-0299

Table of Contents

Starting a School or Classroom Literature Program iv
Teaching Training Suggestions 1
Course Outline/Literature for Children 2
Children's Literature Quotient 4
Classroom Library Selections 7
Meet Judy Blume 9
   Literature Goals 10
   Short-Term Literature Objectives 11
   Pupil Planning 13
   What Makes a Successful Author 14
   Role Reversal 15
   Awards and Medals 16
   Invitations to an Author 19
   Who Is Who in Writing 21
   Letters of Invitation 23
   Letters of Acceptance and Rejection 24
   Resumé 26
   Author News 28
   Thank-You Notes 29
   Speaker's Bureau 30
   A to Z Book Scavenger Hunt 31
   Walkathon for Great Books 32
Iggie's House 35
Otherwise Known as Sheila the Great 48
Then Again, Maybe I Won't 62
Freckle Juice 74
Superfudge 83
Tiger Eyes 96
The One in the Middle Is the Green Kangaroo 109
It's Not the End of the World 119
Just As Long As We're Together 129
Blubber 139
Student-Generated Instruction 150
   Starring Sally J. Freedman as Herself 152
   The Pain and the Great One 157
   Tales of a Fourth Grade Nothing 161
Ideas and Illustrations Supplement—Bulletin Boards 162
Answer Key 171

GA1152

Starting a School or Classroom Literature Program

After evaluating literature programs from across the country, examining literature texts from the leading companies, and working with hundreds of graduate teachers in my children's literature courses, five commonalities appear noticeably in school district literature programs that have been evaluated and graded outstanding. These commonalities are evident from the smallest classroom program to the largest district-wide program and may serve as a starting point for those districts, schools and classrooms that want to increase their commitment to the use of children's literature in their reading and language arts programs.

The first commonality is a highly visible, no doubt in your mind, commitment to good literature both in resources and time. Directed planning time, preservice and in-service programs, updates on new books and a steady diet of local authors, illustrators, librarians and storytellers are found in these programs. This commitment is not just in the first year of the new program, either. Successful programs, even in the poorest districts, have managed to scratch and crawl their way to milking every idea, group and agency for books for children.

Secondly, is a teacher that loves literature and cares about meeting the needs of every child. My graduate students laughed and called the idea impractical, that school principals, instead of saying it's your turn to teach literature this year or rotating the literature job because everyone likes to teach literature, should have teachers in each grade group submit a brief resumé competing for the literature position. Those teachers that have a good understanding of literature, curriculum and learning styles, use a variety of teaching strategies and manipulatives, have high student expectations, and use every resource available in the school, district and area should then be given the literature positions. These attributes were clearly recognizable in successful teachers of literature.

Point three is that successful programs present attractive settings that stimulate learning. This setting includes a variety of reading material, bulletin boards that teach, resource material, displays of children's work in ongoing literature projects, and areas for small and large group instruction. Many attractive and stimulating rooms were visited by teacher evaluators, but 78 percent gave no indication that "children's literature was in progress."

Everyone gets excited about starting new programs, but this excitement soon dies when students and teachers do not have clear goals and measureable objectives developed before work begins. Immediate reinforcement is a must. Children should see their own progress. Everyone feels good about improvements and good work. This is the fourth condition found in successful literature programs.

The fifth segment of successful programs is that they contain student-directed and teacher-directed activities. Peer teaching and systems that make everyone responsible for everyone's progress help to make a program more successful. It is impossible for teachers to know every book that is of interest to children. Making children become important builds leadership, a better classroom climate and a love of school and literature.

Hopefully, using *Integrating the Literature of Judy Blume in the Classroom* will give increased direction in each of the areas mentioned. The book contains a list of goals and objectives, suggestions for in-service literature formats, book ideas, projects and activities that should make your literature program organization run easier and a little bit smoother.

GA1152

Teacher Training Suggestions

The in-service course that follows is designed to give greater direction to the staff development needs of local school districts. If it cannot be taught in its entirety, then a seminar series of guest lecturers (one to a topic) could easily be arranged. Many of the topics, such as Bibliotherapy and Hooking the Reluctant Reader, would make excellent faculty and parent meeting topics. The course is open-ended so local topics of importance can easily be added as a new module or an expansion of an existing module. The pretest that follows is a good evaluative tool in determining what modules should receive emphasis.

GA1152

Course Outline/Literature for Children   Module Format

I. Getting started
   A. Course overview/how children's literature can be integrated into religious and educational settings
   B. Discussion of area research facilities and research techniques
   C. Making literature a larger part of our daily lives
   D. Group discussion of literature in local religious and educational use
   E. Philosophies of use of books

II. The marriage of pupil/books
   A. Motivating students to read be it educational, cultural or religious
   B. What is a "good book"? (words to illustrations)
   C. Storytelling and reading aloud—cultures passed orally
   D. Books and authors

III. Many uses of books
   A. Using books to teach basic skills, values, thinking
   B. Using books to increase student creativity, imagination and self-concept
   C. Using books to enhance research, critical thinking
   D. Activities to develop proficiency with reading books
   E. Peer sharing

IV. Building your classroom library
   A. Biographies and autobiographies
   B. Pourquoi (why) stories
   C. Mysteries, historical and religious essays
   D. Science fiction, fantasy, myths
   E. Resource books

V. Bibliotherapy
   A. What is bibliotherapy?
   B. Using books to solve problems (physical, emotional)
   C. Best-loved characters in children's literature (discussion)
   D. Using books as counseling tools
   E. Books for every situation (discussion)

VI. Maximizing the use of a classroom library
   A. Proper book selection for teachers and students
   B. Using the library for research techniques
   C. Reference materials and their use

VII. Book techniques (using books to teach)
   A. Spelling, comprehension, word recognition
   B. Handwriting, linguistics, phonics, languages
   C. Critical and creative thinking
   D. Speaking

GA1152

VIII. Book writing
  A. Review of Newbery books
  B. Review of Caldecott books
  C. Getting students started on writing books (journals, diaries, letters)
  D. Outlets for children's writing
  E. The writing process

IX. Poetry (religious, cultural, educational)
  A. Developing a climate for poetry
  B. Ideas for poetry—review of poetry books
  C. Teaching figurative language (similes, metaphors)
  D. Verse forms (haiku, couplets, quatrains, psalms, limericks)

X. Small group discussions
  A. Ideas for hooking the reluctant reader
  B. Does sustained silent reading work?
  C. Do good books make good readers, or do good readers read good books?
  D. Is reading a large enough part of religious and secular life? Why? Why not?

XI. Bringing books to life
  A. Book exhibits—creative dramatics
  B. Dull book trials/three-prop poetry
  C. Ethnic luncheons/dialogue of characters
  D. Favorite character dress-up day/religious, educational
  E. Making book reports more enjoyable and meaningful
  F. Peer sharing

XII. Classroom management and organization
  A. Peer presentation "What does research say about classroom reading organization?"
  B. Organizing a school reading program
  C. Reading teacher responsibilities
  D. Time-savers for the classroom teacher
  E. Graded and nontraditional classrooms

XIII. Literature enhancement
  A. Movies, films, VCR (school district, library, phone company, rental stores, local business, reading councils)
  B. Books on tape program
  C. Plays and contests (Olympics of the Mind, etc.), are they worth the effort?
  D. Using outside speakers in the classroom/speaker's bureaus
  E. Peer sharing

XIV. Developing a school literature program for public and religious institutions
  A. Needs assessment
  B. The supervisor/librarian
  C. Parent training involvement, making books and book lists available
  D. Teaching bulletin boards/creative homework
  E. Administrating a school/district program

GA1152

Children's Literature Quotient

A. Place the author's letter next to the book he/she authored.

1. The Great Gilly Hopkins _____
2. Ira Sleeps Over _____
3. A Swiftly Tilting Planet _____
4. Honey, I Love _____
5. Tiger Eyes _____
6. The Tenth Good Thing About Barney _____
7. Sadako and the Thousand Paper Cranes _____
8. Outside over There _____
9. Ramona Quimby—Age 8 _____
10. Chilly Billy _____
11. Leo the Late Bloomer _____

A. Maurice Sendak
B. Peter Mayle
C. Judith Viorst
D. Beverly Cleary
E. Judy Blume
F. Robert Kraus
G. Katherine Paterson
H. Eloise Greenfield
I. Madeleine L'Engle
J. Eleanor Coerr
K. Bernard Waber

B. List two literary works by each of these writers.

1. Shel Silverstein _____
2. Lewis Carroll _____
3. Edgar Allen Poe _____
4. E.B. White _____
5. Mark Twain _____
6. Judy Blume _____
7. Kenneth Koch _____
8. Your choice _____
9. Your choice _____
10. Your choice _____

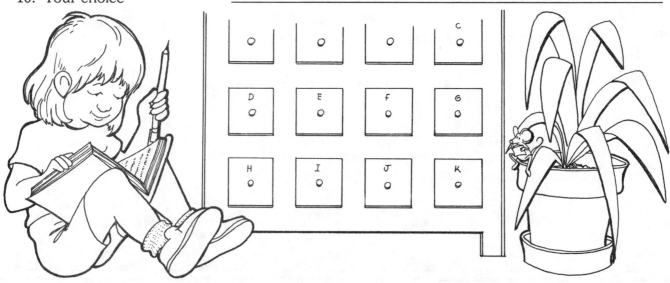

GA1152

C. Name one Newbery and one Caldecott award-winning book (author/illustrator) title.

Newbery: _____

Caldecott: _____

D. Define these terms.

1. limerick _____
   _____

2. rebus _____
   _____

3. portmanteau words _____
   _____

4. pourquoi stories _____
   _____

5. alliteration _____
   _____

6. assonance _____
   _____

7. enjambment _____
   _____

8. onomatopoeia _____
   _____

9. simile _____
   _____

10. haiku _____
   _____

GA1152

AWARD

E. Describe a literary work that has been particularly significant to your life or to the children you teach.

_____

_____

_____

_____

_____

_____

_____

_____

_____

F. You have been asked to organize a classroom/schoolwide literature program in a school where no such program exists. What type of steps would you take to begin and enrich such a program?

_____

_____

_____

_____

_____

_____

_____

_____

_____

G. What type of activities do you expect from this in-service program? Course? Lesson?

_____

_____

_____

_____

_____

_____

_____

_____

_____

GA1152

Classroom Library Selections

There are thousands of exciting books that should be in every teacher's classroom lending library. The ninety-two books that follow provide a small view of a divergent multi-level classroom library. The teacher's text by Barbara Pilon is used as one of the sources at the graduate level. The Katherine Paterson book is one of the better books by an author explaining her craft. A literature program based on "what makes a great book" allows the classroom teacher a greater latitude in the level of the books that are selected for classroom use. The Walkathon for Great Books activity found later in the book will give you an idea for raising money to expand your classroom library.

1. Brown, Janet F., ed., *Curriculum Planning for Young Children*, Washington: National Association for Young Children, 1982.
2. Dorsett, Lyle, ed., *C.S. Lewis Letters to Children*, New York: Macmillan Publishing Company, 1985.
3. Hooper, Walter, ed., *On Stories and Other Essays on Literature*, New York: Harcourt Brace Jovanovich, 1982.
4. Paterson, Katherine, *Gates of Excellence (On Reading and Writing Books for Children)*, New York: Elsevier/Nelson Books, 1981.
5. *Pilon, A. Barbara, *Teaching Language Arts Creatively in the Elementary Grades*, New York: John Wiley and Sons, 1978.

Title	Author
6. The Shadowmaker	Ron Hanson
7. If There Were Dreams to Sell	Barbara Lalicki
8. There's a Nightmare in My Closet	Mercer Mayer
9. Spectacles	Ann Beattie
10. Hugh Pine and the Good Place	Janwillen Van De Wetering
11. Goose Eggs	E. J. Taylor
12. Stopping by Woods on a Snowy Evening	Robert Frost
13. Two Under Par	Kevin Henkes
14. Even Higher	Barbara Cohen
15. The Strawflower	Hilde Heyduck-Huth
16. Beauty and the Beast	Deborah Apy
17. The Reluctant Dragon	Kenneth Grahame
18. The Tooth Witch	Nurit Karlin
19. I'll Always Love You	Hans Wilhelm
20. Alphabears	Kathleen Hague
21. On Market Street	Anita/Arnold Lobel
22. A Three Hat Day	Laura Geringer
23. The Zapped Z	Chris Van Allsburg
24. The Phantom Tollbooth	Norton Juster
25. Honey, I Love	Eloise Greenfield
26. Tight Times	Barbara Shook Hazen
27. The Wreck of the Zephyr	Chris Van Allsburg
28. The Acorn People	Ron Jones
29. Can I Keep Him	Steven Kellogg
30. The Summer of the Swans	Betsy Byars
31. If I Ruled the World	Judith Viorst
32. Bea and Mr. Jones	Amy Schwartz
33. The Wonderful Word of Henry Sugar	Roald Dahl
34. The Cat Ate My Gymsuit	Paula Danziger
35. East of the Sun—West of the Moon	Mercer Mayer
36. Where the Wild Things Are	Maurice Sendak
37. Outside over There	Maurice Sendak
38. I Wish I Had a Computer That Makes Waffles	Fitzhugh Dodson
39. On Beyond Zebra	Dr. Seuss

*The author's Integrating Literature into L.A. Programs Bible

GA1152

40.	The Lorax	Dr. Seuss
41.	Tiger Eyes	Judy Blume
42.	If I Were in Charge of the World	Judith Viorst
43.	Where the Sidewalk Ends	Shel Silverstein
44.	A Light in the Attic	Shel Silverstein
45.	Leo the Late Bloomer	Robert Kraus
46.	The Children's Story	James Clavell
47.	Ramona Quimby—Age 8	Beverly Cleary
48.	Count Worm	Roger Hargreaves
49.	Albert the Alphabetical Elephant	Roger Hargreaves
50.	Ira Sleeps Over	Bernard Waber
51.	Jacob Have I Loved	Katherine Paterson
52.	Bridge to Terabithia	Katherine Paterson
53.	Encyclopedia Brown	Donald Sobol
54.	The Trumpet of the Swan	E.B. White
55.	Professor Diggins Dragons	Felice Holman
56.	A Fly Went By	Mike McClintock
57.	Just for You	Mercer Mayer
58.	Just Me and My Dad	Mercer Mayer
59.	Little Monster's Alphabet Book	Mercer Mayer
60.	From the Mixed Up Files of Basil E. Frankweiler	E.L. Konigsburg
61.	The Chocolate Touch	Patrick Catling
62.	Keep Your Mouth Closed Dear	Aliki
63.	The King Who Rained	Fred Gwynne
64.	Choose Your Own Adventure (Sahara)	D. Terman
65.	A Wrinkle in Time	Madeleine L'Engle
66.	Sadako and the Thousand Paper Cranes	Eleanor Coerr
67.	Friends of the Loony Lake Monster	Frank Bonham
68.	Cloudy with a Chance of Meatballs	Judi Barrett
69.	Drummer Hoff	Barbara Emberley
70.	Jumanji	Chris Van Allsburg
71.	Faint Frogs Feeling Feverish	Lilian Obligado
72.	May I Bring a Friend	Beatrice DeRegniers
73.	A Visit to William Blake's Inn	Nancy Willard
74.	The Fool of the World and the Flying Ship	Arthur Ransome
75.	Alexander and the Terrible, Horrible, No Good, Very Bad Day	Judith Viorst
76.	The Gorilla Did It	Barbara Shook Hazen
77.	The Velveteen Rabbit	Margery Williams
78.	Notes from a Different Drummer	Barbara Baskin
79.	The Magic of Lewis Carroll	John Fisher
80.	The Horse in Harry's Room	Syd Hoff
81.	Amelia Bedelia	Peggy Parish
82.	The Little Red Lighthouse and the Great Gray Bridge	Hildegarde Swift
83.	My Darling, My Hamburger	Paul Zindel
84.	Mrs. Frisby and the Rats of NIMH	Robert C. O'Brien
85.	Island of the Blue Dolphins	Scott O'Dell
86.	Charlie and the Chocolate Factory	Roald Dahl
87.	Chocolate Fever	Robert Kimmel Smith
88.	The Witch of Blackbird Pond	Elizabeth George Speare
89.	The House with a Clock in Its Walls	John Bellairs
90.	The Grounding of Group Six	Julian F. Thompson
91.	A Swiftly Tilting Planet	Madeleine L'Engle
92.	The Puzzler's Paradise	Helene Hovanec

Meet
Judy Blume

Literature Goals

Integrating the Literature of Judy Blume in the Classroom was written with particular classroom goals and objectives in mind. These goals and objectives are designed to give increased direction to literature programs, make teacher lesson planning easier and to help give specific information when reporting to parents. These goals and objectives also give teachers a framework for designing individual educational plans (IEP's) for students who will be using this book as part of their everyday school program. It is the hope of the author that these goals and objectives will be expanded by the teachers who use this book.

Annual Goals

Integrating the Literature of Judy Blume in the Classroom and covered readings can be used to:

1. expand student reading repertoires
2. research the background of authors and illustrators
3. analyze current events
4. develop the short story
5. build the components of lead and minor characters
6. develop creative and critical thinking
7. generate computer science literature files
8. expose students to video techniques
9. develop an understanding of the world community
10. analyze the foundations of relationships
11. learn advanced writing skills
12. experiment with public speaking/acting
13. evaluate and critique one's own ideas
14. institute encounters with creative people
15. give experiences with multi-media
16. enter creative competitions and contests
17. bolster basic educational skills
18. create short and long-term projects
19. amplify environmental concerns
20. show cause and effect relationships
21. develop a sensitivity to beauty, feelings, love, truth, justice, faith and human qualities
22. create parent and educator speaker's bureaus
23. investigate inventors, literary and historical figures
24. expose students to literary, educational and cultural resources
25. enrich student backgrounds in the arts (dance, art, music and theater)

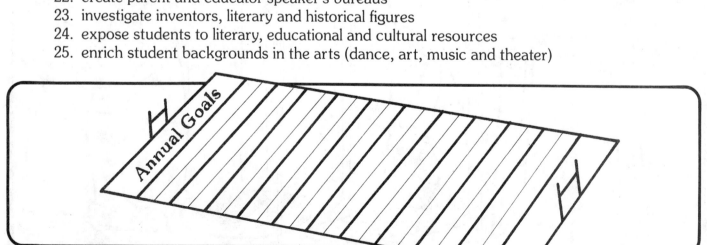

GA1152

Short-Term Literature Objectives

Annual goals and short-term objectives form the basis of a good literature program. When stating your short-term objectives, be specific. This will give the needed direction to begin your projects. It also gives you a foundation for your post project evaluation. There are hundreds of objectives that could be written. These objectives are representative of the directions that projects can take before and after exposure to creative literature.

Short-Term Objectives

Integrating the Literature of Judy Blume in the Classroom and selected readings can be used to meet the following short-term objectives:

1. After studying community problems, I will create a multi-media presentation highlighting solutions to two selected problems.

2. After studying creative contributors to a selected area of interest/study, I will design a poster emphasizing the individual and his contribution.

3. After studying three lead characters appearing in Judy Blume books, I will create a split page analysis of one of the characters with my favorite character from another book.

4. After studying the four areas of creativity, I will pick four book characters who exhibit these traits, draw their bodies and highlight the traits next to them.

5. After investigating filmstrip techniques, I will create a teaching filmstrip for one of our selected readings.

6. After examining my classmates' journals, portfolios and projects, I will create a directory of outlets for children's products.

7. After identifying my best projects, writings, skills and ideas, I will enter a creative competition or investigate being published . . . spelling bee, article writing, science bowl, future problem-solving contest, the stock market game, real estate hunt, olympics of the mind or new inventions contest.

8. After studying everyday law and the situations in my reading that might warrant a knowledge of law—separation, divorce, adoption, children's rights—I will present a real or imaginary case with points of view and actual outcomes.

 GA1152

9. After studying creative characters in literature, I will create a five-member hall of fame displaying each member's characteristics in a diorama, model, poster or 3-D display.

10. After studying how computer science can be used to enhance our literature program, I will use our word processor (Appleworks, Mecc Writer, etc.) to create a file of my favorite books, characters and situations. I will use the centering, tab, underlining and bold face modes to add to the appearance of my work.

11. After surveying the reading and literature needs of my school and community, I will do five hours of community service in the area of reading/literature.

12. After reading three Judy Blume (or other author) selections, I will participate in the Adopt a Book program that will culminate with my design of an advertising campaign to attract people to my selection.

13. After researching three children's literature illustrators, I will take one Judy Blume book and illustrate its cover in the style of each of the three illustrators (three book covers).

14. After practicing photography techniques, I will create an autobiographical snapshot diary/journal.

15. After studying places that books can take you, I will design a travel poster for one of the settings in a Judy Blume story.

16. After studying the art of exaggeration, I will exaggerate two events from my reading and minimize two others.

17. After discussions with my classmates, I will complete a mini essay on three ideas to make our literature program more exciting.

18. After studying video techniques, I will make a video of a scene or problem from one of our selections.

19. After documenting classroom teaching techniques, I will present a fifteen-minute literature activity, discussion or drill on one of our selected readings.

GA1152

Pupil Planning
Goals and Objectives

This pupil planning sheet has been developed to support your school literature program, this book and any of your selected readings for this year. It is designed to make you pre-think the direction you will take before beginning your literature or book assignments. Please select three books that you will be reading this year. Review the annual goals and short-term data sheets before selecting four from each category. Write two goals and objectives of your own that will parallel your selections. Try to set a date when each objective will be completed. Complete your choices in the spaces provided below. Attach this sheet to your literature notebook.

A. My three book selections (titles and authors) are

    1. _____

    2. _____

    3. _____

B. The four annual goals I have chosen for my work are

    1. _____

    2. _____

    3. _____

    4. _____

C. My short-term objectives will be

    1. _____

    2. _____

    3. _____

    4. _____

D. The two annual goals and short-term objectives that I would like to add are

Goals:

    1. _____

    2. _____

Objectives:

    1. _____

    2. _____

Which direction will you take?

GA1152

What Makes a Successful Author

Judy Blume is read by millions of children all over the world. Her books have made us laugh and cry. Through the magic of her writing, she has taken us from Atlantic City, New Jersey, to the shores of California. We have visited big cities, the suburbs and small towns. She has helped us understand friendship, loneliness, separation, divorce, death, happiness, grown-ups and growing up. She has made us realize that most of our problems have been experienced by others and just like her characters, we can find solutions to many of them.

This could have been the brief description of Judy Blume that appeared on any number of her book covers. It makes us think and see the scope of her writing, but it really doesn't tell us any real information about Judy Blume. Who, then, is Judy Blume? Maybe some of these questions will allow you to look at Judy Blume, the person, a little more closely. Maybe you will use some of these same questions to examine the authors of other books that you have read.

1. What do you think Judy Blume's childhood was like?

2. Do you think that she experienced all the problems she talks about in her stories?

3. Do you think her childhood was a happy one?

4. How much of her own children do you think she reflects in each of her writings?

5. Why does she talk about struggling families, sibling rivalry, divorce, death, sexual awareness and lost friends in so many of her books?

6. What writers and storytellers do you think influenced her writings and life?

7. Where can we go to get some solid inside information about her?

8. What other authors would you compare to her? How did you make this determination?

Role Reversal

If you were a successful writer, on what topics would you focus in the following situations? Pick four situations from those below that you can creatively develop in your writing.

1. Your school classroom
2. Your home
3. Dealing with brothers and sisters
4. Dealing with your parents
5. Taking care of your pets
6. At the doctor's office
7. On your vacation
8. Watching your body change
9. Being a good friend
10. Something that would make people laugh
11. Something that would make people feel sorry for you
12. In a car, train or plane
13. Camping in the yard
14. In your apartment's elevator or stairway

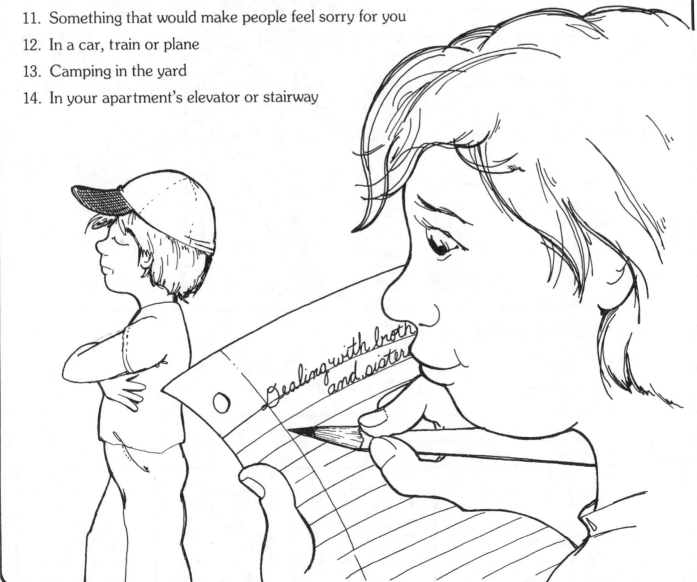

GA1152

Student Award Nominations

The Newbery and Caldecott awards are presented each year for the best book and best illustrations. Some all-time classics have been honored by the committees that vote on and present these awards. Give some of the past Newbery and Caldecott winners your best inspection. Find out what the judging criteria includes. Determine in your own mind what made them special. Focus on some aspects of these books that may have appealed to other reviewers, but not to you.

Classroom Elections for Book and Illustrator of the Year

Select five books that you would like to nominate for this year's Caldecott and Newbery awards. Place the best one of the five in nomination for your classroom's award. Give a presentation to your classmates as to why your book should be selected for such an honor.

Caldecott Nominations

1. _____
2. _____
3. _____
4. _____
5. _____

Newbery Nominations

1. _____
2. _____
3. _____
4. _____
5. _____

My best of the best award nomination is _____
_____

because (Detail your reasons, please.)

_____
_____
_____
_____

GA1152

Literary Medals

There are many medals presented to authors and illustrators of outstanding books. The Hans Christian Andersen, Newbery and Caldecott awards are three of the most famous. Reproduce and give the significance of two literary honors on this page. On the following page, design a medal called the Judy Blume Medal and describe the parameters of the award. Also name and design an award after yourself. Explain when and to whom it is to be awarded. The author recommends that you design a serious medal and a humorous one after yourself. If you are not a great artist, use cutouts to enhance the appearance of the medals you are designing yourself.

Medal I

Significance

_____

_____

_____

_____

_____

_____

Medal II

Significance

_____

_____

_____

_____

_____

_____

GA1152

Student-Designed Literary Awards

You are on a committee that would like to create a literary honor for an author, artist, editor or publisher. The award is going to be named after Judy Blume. What will it look like (crystal, scroll, medal or statuette)? Place your award in the space below.

A literary honor is being named after you. What did you do in literature to be honored in such a way? What will the award look like?

_____

_____

_____

_____

_____

_____

_____

_____

_____

_____

Mount your awards on larger pieces of paper. Give good descriptions of how the honors are to be awarded.

GA1152

Invitations to an Author

Teacher Directions

This mini unit will help your students explore writers, their products and the world of bringing their works to the public's attention.

1. **Who Is Who in Writing** (page 21). Have the student place a picture of the author on the left-hand side of the book and draw a picture of his favorite work on the right-hand side before filling in the relevant information about each. Since this project will lead into inviting a real life, imaginary or deceased character to school, it need not be limited to just Judy Blume or other authors.

2. **Coming Soon** (page 22). Your students will design a poster announcing that Judy Blume will be coming to school to speak to your class. Your students may announce the arrival of a famous character in literature, history or even the arrival of an historic event—Coming Soon, the Great Flood!

3. **Oh, Please Visit Us** (pages 23-24). Explain to your class that writers get thousands of invitations a year to speak to various groups. Discuss with them a variety of approaches that could be used in a speaking invitation (humor, plea, greatly benefit, love your work, bet you wouldn't come to a small school) letter. Your class will then write to the author. In addition to the author, they will request that he/she bring two book characters along with him when he comes to your school. Remind your class to give specific reasons why you'd like these characters to come along. Historical characters could bring their cohorts with them (Custer/Sitting Bull), also. Page 23 will be used to write a letter of invitation to the author and to a particular character. Page 24 will be an acceptance letter and a rejection letter with three reasons why he/she can/can't speak at your school.

4. **Dreams Come True** (page 25). Discuss with the class the preparations that will be necessary to welcome this historical character or author to your class. An emcee will have to be picked to make comments before and after the speaker's talk. Page 25 will give your class practice in writing introductions, predicting what the guest will talk about and using these predictions to make final comments about the speech. Classes should write, memorize and then give oral introductions of the person or character they have chosen.

GA1152

5. **Author's Resumé** (pages 26-27). Show the class samples of two or three types of resumés. Discuss the purpose of a resumé with them. Have them imagine that they are Judy Blume. What would she put on her resumé? This could be a research project to get the exact information or an exaggerated writing assignment. The blank page (page 27) that follows is for the student to write his own resumé. I have my classes write one for a job now and one for a job when they are twenty-five. Real information in their writing has an *R* in parentheses next to it; imaginary has an *I* next to it.

6. **Author News** (page 28). Have your class brainstorm. Catch-your-eye headings for an author's or historical figure's visit to your school. Have them generate how the newspaper article will look before and after this visit. They will also include three other news stories that would appear next to the author's story. Remind your class that this story might not necessarily appear on the front page and that the style of writing for the book, leisure or entertainment sections is much different from the style of the front page.

7. **Thank You** (page 29). Explain to the class that even though the emcee thanked the speaker in his/her final remarks, it is proper to send a thank-you note to each guest. Each student will do this for the principal speaker and the character he brought along.

8. **Speaker's Bureau** (page 30). Most colleges and universities have lists of people that would come to your school to give presentations. Yet, there are hundreds of qualified people on a variety of topics who do not appear on these lists. Explain to the class that they will be compiling a list of speakers and their topics for a school speaker's bureau. Discuss with them at least five categories in which these people might be listed. Give this as a small group project or individual project.

9. **A to Z Book Scavenger Hunt** (page 31). This is a classroom homework activity. After dividing the class into teams, take the first ten letters of the alphabet and give each student the responsibility for bringing in the most creative items starting with the particular letters chosen. After the students show their objects, the class votes on which team should be given the point. Then follow this up with the work sheet on page 31. Each student chooses one of his favorite books. He then goes on a scavenger hunt finding normal words (1 point), proper nouns (2 points) and characters (3 points), starting with the letters *A* to *Z* (one for each letter). Highest total score is the winner.

10. **Speaker's Bureau** (page 30). Have your class select and vote on possible classroom speakers after completing the Speaker's Bureau information sheet.

GA1152

Who Is Who in Writing

Imagine that the book below is sitting on your bookstore display shelf. You are able to see the author's picture on the back cover and the book title and illustrations on the front. Find a picture of Judy Blume or your favorite author and mount it on your cover. Complete the book title and surrounding illustrations. Complete the information sheet below. Compose a leader for this book.

Figure A   Figure B

Author's name_____

Birth date _____ Birthplace _____

Top five books_____

_____

_____

_____

_____

Favorite book by this author _____

Least favorite book by this author _____

Future topics you think this author should write about _____

_____

_____

_____

_____

Use the back of this paper to highlight the funniest and most serious situations that this author has placed a character in.

Figures A and B are the inside book flaps that contain the leader. Write a leader for this book on the flaps.

Coming Soon

Judy Blume has been invited to speak at your school. Any interested reader of her books may attend. Design a poster announcing her appearance at your school. Be sure to include the date, time and location. Discuss with your classmates the creative techniques you might use to announce her arrival. Write a one-minute radio spot on the back of this paper. Have a classmate time your presentation before reciting it in front of your classmates. Make an announcement flyer for a Judy Blume book that hasn't been written yet. Use this paper to plan your work before transferring your ideas to 8½" x 11" paper.

GA1152

Oh, Please Visit Us
Letters of Invitation

Letter A: Good writers and speakers get hundreds of invitations to speak at schools, seminars, college classes and dinners.

What would you write in a letter to Judy Blume, your favorite author or someone in the news to get him/her to visit your school?

Letter A

Letter B: The second letter is to be written to your favorite character in either a Judy Blume book, your favorite book or an event in history. Try to be sincere, humorous or way out in your approach to get this imaginary character to visit your school.

Letter B

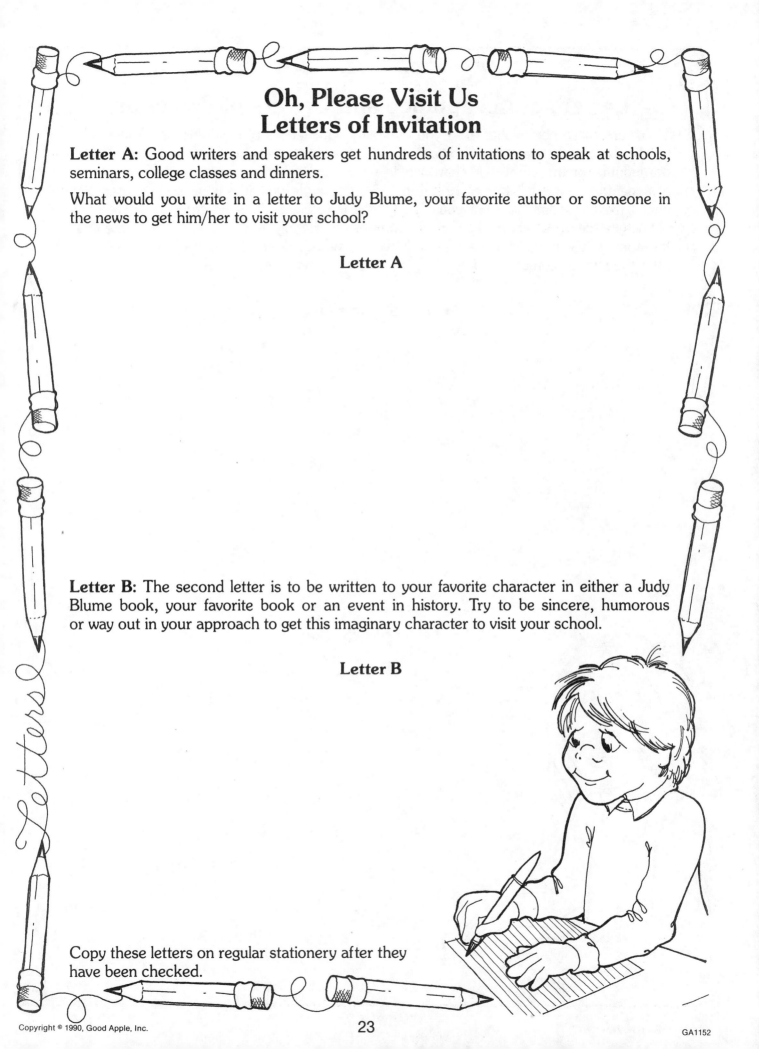

Copy these letters on regular stationery after they have been checked.

GA1152

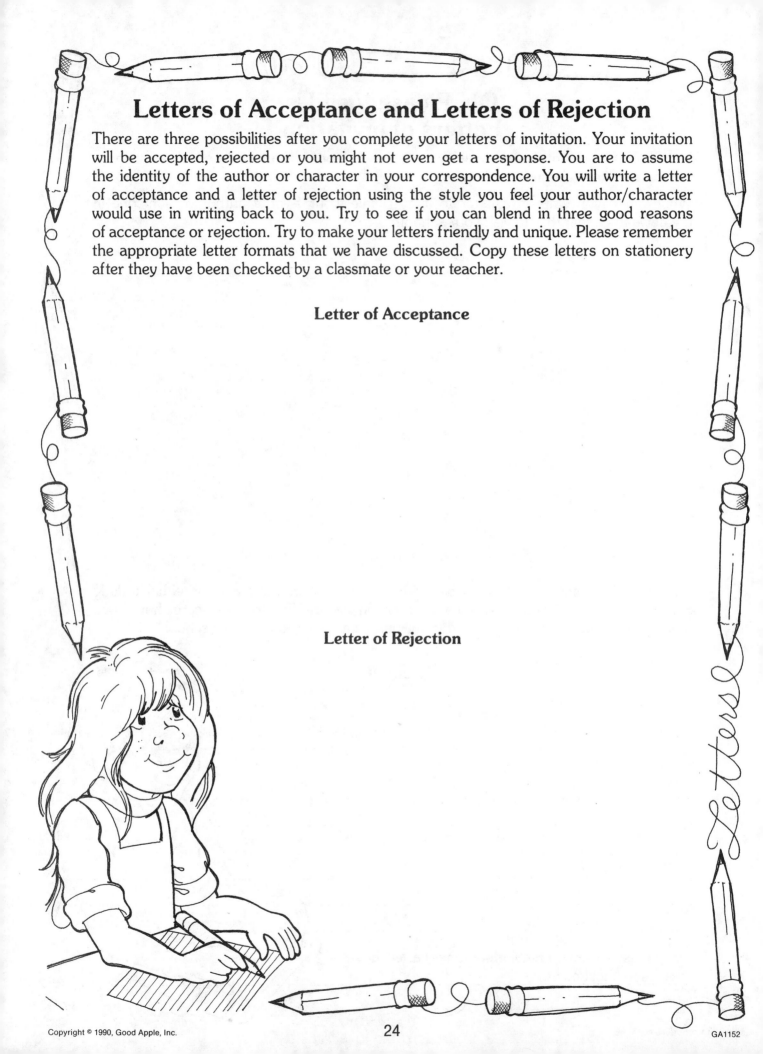

Letters of Acceptance and Letters of Rejection

There are three possibilities after you complete your letters of invitation. Your invitation will be accepted, rejected or you might not even get a response. You are to assume the identity of the author or character in your correspondence. You will write a letter of acceptance and a letter of rejection using the style you feel your author/character would use in writing back to you. Try to see if you can blend in three good reasons of acceptance or rejection. Try to make your letters friendly and unique. Please remember the appropriate letter formats that we have discussed. Copy these letters on stationery after they have been checked by a classmate or your teacher.

Letter of Acceptance

Letter of Rejection

GA1152

Dreams Come True

Judy Blume or the character you have selected has accepted your invitation to speak at your school. You have won the honor of being the emcee and must introduce the speaker.

A. What will you say in your introduction and what accomplishments of your speaker will you highlight?

_____
_____
_____
_____
_____
_____
_____
_____

B. What do you think the most important points of your speaker's presentation will be?

_____
_____
_____
_____
_____
_____
_____
_____
_____
_____

C. A good emcee's closing remarks should mention some key points of your presenter's speech, a wish for continued success and possibly a request for a return visit. Compose your remarks below.

_____
_____
_____
_____
_____
_____
_____
_____

GA1152

Invitations to an Author—Resumé

A resumé is a formal form that gives an accurate but brief description of your interests and work qualifications. It gives your future employer the chance to see where you have been, what you have done and what your future successes might be. Many employers also ask for a portfolio containing samples of your best work. What do you think Judy Blume's resumé would look like if she were applying for the job of librarian in your school?

Resumé for _____, School Librarian

Name _____

Address _____

_____

_____

Phone Number _____

Social Security Number _____

Highest Degree Held _____

_____

Additional Degrees _____

_____

_____

Expected Salary _____

Awards _____

_____

_____

Publications _____

_____

_____

_____

Future Goals _____

_____

_____

_____

Job Experience (most recent to least recent)
(Student Hint: Remember to put facts down that are related to the job for which you are applying.)
Please use the back.

GA1152

Blank Resumé—Judy Blume Follow-Up

You are now twenty-five years old. You are about to apply for a job that you have been training/ schooling/working for for years. After giving us a description of the job, complete the resume form provided below. Please add the additional categories that you feel are needed to give the best description of your professional experience.

Job Description _____

Job Title _____

Name _____

Address _____

_____

Phone Number _____

Social Security Number _____

Highest Degree Held _____

_____

Additional Schooling _____

_____

_____

Expected Salary _____

Awards _____

_____

_____

Publications _____

_____

_____

_____

Future Goals _____

_____

_____

_____

Job Experience (most recent to least recent) Please use the back of the paper if necessary.

_____

_____

_____

_____

_____

GA1152

Author News

Below you will find a page representing the leisure, entertainment, book review or front section of a newspaper. There is room for four articles. One of the articles should announce a visit of Judy Blume, a book character or historical figure to your school. The other three sections will reflect news that might also appear on such a page. Make your headlines witty and eye-catching. Your stories should be brief and contain the who, what, why, when, where and how formats used in most newspaper stories. Combine the pages of classmates (who are writing about different people) into a mini newspaper.

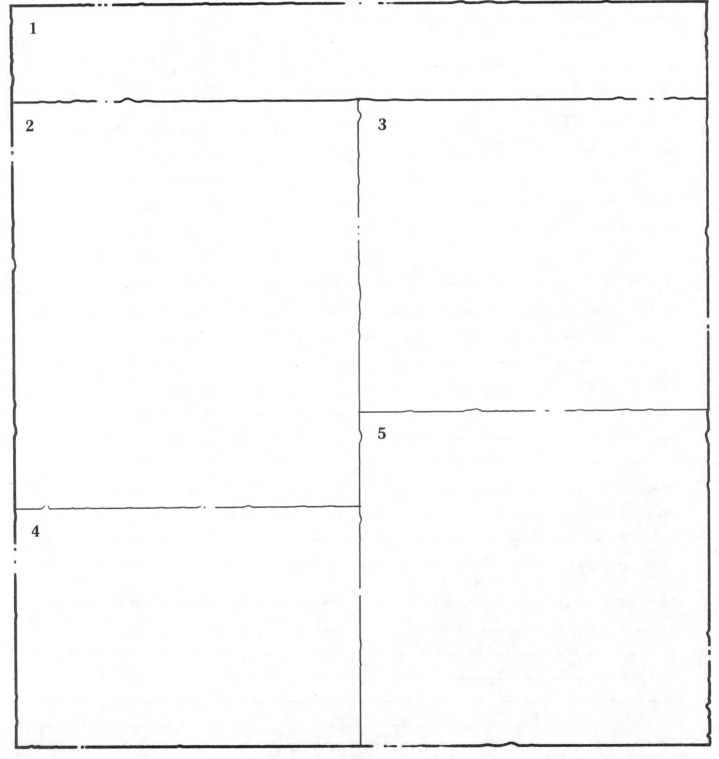

Thank-You Notes

Use the two letter outlines below to write thank-you notes to Judy Blume, one of her book characters or the historical character that you chose to invite to your classroom. Highlight the benefit your classmates derived from their visit to your school. Try to give your letters the light, personal touch that letters of this kind have. Copy these letters on stationery and make a display bulletin board for your letters and your classmates' letters.

Thank-You Note to Judy Blume

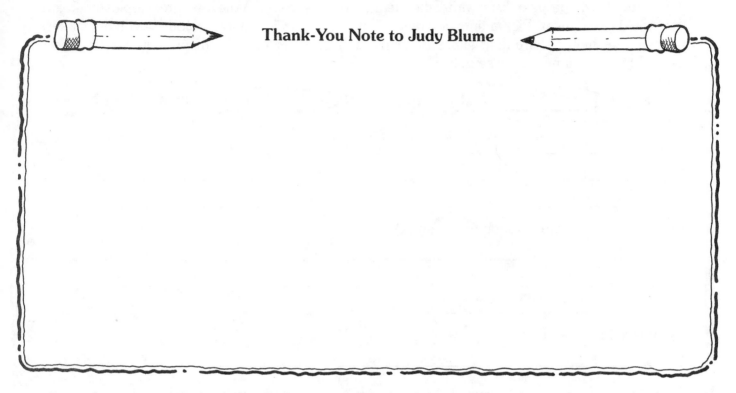

Thank-You Note to Book Character/Historical Figure

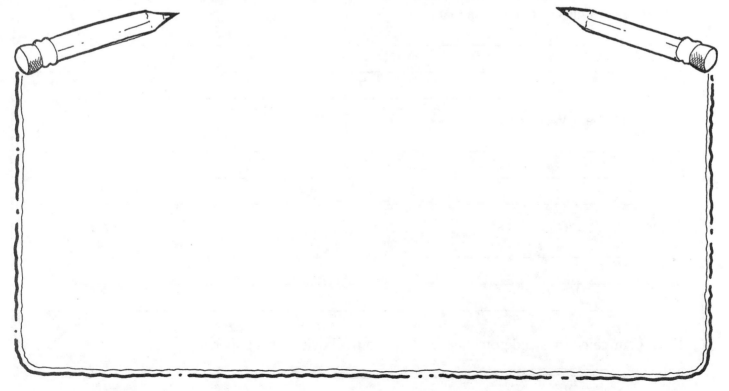

GA1152

Speaker's Bureau

Most colleges and universities have a speaker's bureau. It is a listing of speakers and the subjects/topics that they can discuss with interested organizations. Your town probably has many well-known and lesser known, but just as able, speakers that might be willing to speak at your school. Pick two teammates. Find three people in each category below who might be available to speak at your school. Pick topics you think your classmates might be interested in learning more about. Merge your lists with other teams in your room. Vote on three topics/speakers that you'd like to hear. Pick a time and date. Write a letter of invitation to your selected speakers to see if they would share their expertise with your class. Discuss who might fit in each category below before beginning your search.

Name   **Topic**   **Contact Number**

Authors, Writers or Poets

1. _____

2. _____

3. _____

Artists (paint, sculpture, wood or ceramics)

1. _____

2. _____

3. _____

Scientists and Inventors

1. _____

2. _____

3. _____

Government Officials (local, regional or state)

1. _____

2. _____

3. _____

Family Members/World Travelers

1. _____

2. _____

3. _____

Entertainers/Sports Figures

1. _____

2. _____

3. _____

Place your categories and potential speakers on the back of this paper.

                                                 GA1152

A to Z Book Scavenger Hunt

You are about to go on an A to Z scavenger hunt through three of your favorite books. The highest score at the end of the activity is the winner. You are to write one word from your books for each letter listed below. Points are given in the following manner: 1 point for a normal word; 2 points for a proper noun; 3 points for the name of a character in your books. Please put the titles and authors of the three books you are using below.

1. _____

2. _____

3. _____

Refer to them by number next to each word you find, so we can tell in which of the three books you found that particular word.

Word	Book Number	Points Scored
A. _____	_____	_____
B. _____	_____	_____
C. _____	_____	_____
D. _____	_____	_____
E. _____	_____	_____
F. _____	_____	_____
G. _____	_____	_____
H. _____	_____	_____
I. _____	_____	_____
J. _____	_____	_____
K. _____	_____	_____
L. _____	_____	_____
M. _____	_____	_____
N. _____	_____	_____
O. _____	_____	_____
P. _____	_____	_____
Q. _____	_____	_____
R. _____	_____	_____
S. _____	_____	_____
T. _____	_____	_____
U. _____	_____	_____
V. _____	_____	_____
W. _____	_____	_____
X. _____	_____	_____
Y. _____	_____	_____
Z. _____	_____	_____

You may pick two classmates, each using one book, to complete this activity.

GA1152

Walkathon for Great Books

The activities in this book center around twelve Judy Blume books. They were designed to be open-ended. This means they are adaptable to any literature series. Few libraries and bookstores have all the books that we generally look for during a school year. Most, though, have a system that will locate the books you need, as well as the twelve books which are the basis for this book. If you want to make these books and additional books part of your classroom library, the walkathon for great books might be the answer.

The walkathon operates the same way that the March of Dimes Walkathon works. You can pick a school athletic track, large field or just walk around the outside of your school. One of our local preschool programs did this. The four-year-old winner walked around his building fifty times. He was so tired that his parents reported he slept for two straight days. Before walking, you will ask people to sponsor you. They do this by pledging a penny, nickel, dime or more, depending on the size of the accomplishment. The pledgee then donates the money for each time you walk around the prescribed area. If you walk around it five times and that person pledged five cents, you then collect a quarter. If you have this same deal with twenty people, you now have added five dollars to your classroom library fund. If your class has twenty students, that comes to one hundred dollars. This is more than enough to purchase the twelve books and additional selections.

It sounds simple, but organizing a literature walkathon takes a lot of effort and cooperation. The two pages that follow will help you to organize your committees, contact local newspapers and radio stations, write articles for your school newspaper, make posters, have refreshments and first aid at the walk site, recruit collectors at the site and generate school and community support for your project.

Make a list with your teacher and classmates of the books that you would like to have in your classroom. Try to pick books that aren't readily available in your area. Divide your class into book selection committees. Have each committee nominate books in their particular selection area (literature classics, new books, award winners, how-to books, research, newspapers, journals or magazines). Have your class vote on the selections from each group. List your final choices and their costs. Give your list to a local bookstore. If you buy all your books from one store, you should get an additional discount.

GA1152

Walkathon for Great Books

You will need the following committees to have a successful literature walkathon. Ask your classmates to volunteer for the jobs. Try to arrange it so everyone serves on a committee. No one should serve on more than two committees. Feel free to add or combine committees as you see fit. Remember to set time schedules for all projects and committee work. It is also advisable to have checkpoints where everyone can report on his progress and request additional help if he finds the task calls for it. Remember to clear all work with your teacher before beginning your assignments. A mini plan might serve this purpose.

Our chairperson for the walkathon is _____.

Site Selection Committee

1. _____
2. _____
3. _____

Banking/Collection Committee

1. _____
2. _____
3. _____

Art/Advertising Committee

1. _____
2. _____
3. _____

Correspondence Committee

1. _____
2. _____
3. _____

Newspaper Committee

1. _____
2. _____
3. _____

Refreshment Committee

1. _____
2. _____
3. _____

First Aid

1. _____
2. _____
3. _____

Parent Assistance Committee

1. _____
2. _____
3. _____

Volunteer Collectors Committee

1. _____
2. _____
3. _____

Radio/TV Committee

1. _____
2. _____
3. _____

GA1152

Walkathon for Great Books Recording Sheet
General Letter Form

Dear Lover of Good Literature,

As part of my classroom's effort to increase our literature library, I am participating in the Walkathon for Great Books.

This money-raising event challenges me to walk _____.

I feel I can do this approximately _____ times.

I am asking people in my family and community to sponsor me by donating money for each _____ that is completed.

Please help us reach our goal by donating.

One cent a _____ donators

1. _____
2. _____
3. _____
4. _____
5. _____

Five cents a _____ donators

1. _____
2. _____
3. _____
4. _____
5. _____

Ten cents a _____ donators

1. _____
2. _____
3. _____
4. _____
5. _____

Good luck with your effort.

1. _____
2. _____
3. _____

General Donations

Amount _____

Amount _____

Amount _____

GA1152

Iggie's House

Freedom for Turtles Club

New Kids on the Block

Multi-Cultural Neighborhoods

Respect

Friendship

WELCOME NEIGHBORS

Lead-Ins to Literature

Winifred Bates Barringer is a one-woman dynamo and the self-appointed welcome wagon of her block. Her best friend Iggie has moved away. The family that moves into Iggie's house is the first black family on an all-white block. Iggie begins a campaign to win the friendship of the three children in the family (Tina, Glenn and Herbie). She makes mistakes and has some successes.

Before you read *Iggie's House*, see if you can predict some of the things that a good writer might develop while using this theme of lost friend, new neighbors.

1. What points do you think the writer will develop in this story?

   _____

   _____

2. Do you think the story will take place in the country or city? Would it make a difference in the city or country?

   _____

   _____

3. What types of activities will the children be involved in?

   _____

   _____

4. Will their parents be involved in the story? How?

   _____

   _____

5. Can you write an opening paragraph before you read the story?

   _____

   _____

6. What kind of problems will the author insert in the story?

   _____

   _____

7. Draw a cover for this book before reading it. After reading the book, place a new cover next to your first cover.

   _____

   _____

Vexing Vocabulary I

Use each italicized word in a sentence of your own that shows you understand the word's meaning. Rewrite each sentence with a word similar in meaning to the italicized word.

1. Gum popping even with sugarless gum is *disgusting*.

_____

_____

2. Winnie's *opinion* wasn't always listened to.

_____

_____

3. Winnie *wandered* all over the house.

_____

_____

4. The Detroit *riot* was very destructive.

_____

_____

5. Her handling of the situation was *awful*.

_____

_____

6. Tina *hollered* about being left behind.

_____

_____

7. They worked for Smith, *Incorporated*.

_____

_____

8. Glenn was caught *gnawing* at his nails.

_____

_____

9. What would make this *petition* easier to understand?

_____

_____

10. The cat caused a real *commotion* in the yard.

_____

_____

What ten words would you suggest adding to this list of "should know" words from *Iggie's House*?

1. _____   4. _____   7. _____   9. _____

2. _____   5. _____   8. _____   10. _____

3. _____   6. _____

Select a partner and give each other practice trying to spell the words from both lists.

Vexing Vocabulary II

escaped	especially	cringed
smudged	disgusting	squiggly
bitter	riot	curvy
shrugged	glum	interrupted
stoop	gritted	allergy
giggled	perspiration	compliment
holler	blah	ghetto
Tokyo	Myrna	questionnaire

Copy each vocabulary word to the left of the twenty-four lines below. Follow your teacher's directions as he/she instructs you to write a sentence of your own using each word. The author prefers that the student find the actual sentence in the story where each word appears. This is cumbersome, at first, but necessary for realizing what relationship the vocabulary word has to the story. It also beats writing the word three times, then writing it in a sentence, then writing it in a paragraph for review. After completing this activity, turn to the back vocabulary section of the book where you will find forty-eight creative ways to follow up this assignment. Pick two activities that are challenging to you and complete them on a separate sheet of paper.

1. _____
2. _____
3. _____
4. _____
5. _____
6. _____
7. _____
8. _____
9. _____
10. _____
11. _____
12. _____
13. _____
14. _____
15. _____
16. _____
17. _____
18. _____
19. _____
20. _____
21. _____
22. _____
23. _____
24. _____

GA1152

Just the Facts

1. How old is Winnie? _____ Tina? _____

2. What grade is Glenn in? _____ Herbie? _____

3. Where did Iggie move? _____

4. What city did the Garber's come from? _____

5. Whose mother was called Germs Incorporated? _____

6. What are two definitions for the word *riot* ?

   A. _____
   _____

   B. _____
   _____

7. What mistake did Tina make with the No-Shed?

   _____

8. What does Aunt Myrna do while Winnie is at the pool? _____

9. Who did Winnie ask to fill out her questionnaire at the pool? _____

10. Why did the kids say "good riddance" to the Germ family? _____
    _____

List five questions that you would ask about the story *Iggie's House*.

1. _____
2. _____
3. _____
4. _____
5. _____

GA1152

What's Your Opinion?

1. How do you think Iggie felt about moving once again?

_____

_____

2. Do you think first impressions are important? Explain.

_____

_____

3. Why do you think Herbie was so untrusting?

_____

_____

4. Was Winnie a good friend or just a do-gooder?

_____

_____

5. What would you have done to make the Garber family feel more comfortable in their new home?

_____

_____

6. What do you think was the most interesting characteristic of each of the principal characters?

_____

_____

7. How could Winnie have made her questionnaire more meaningful?

_____

_____

8. Could the Landon family have resolved their problem without moving?

_____

_____

Add five good What's Your Opinion questions to this sheet. Put a star next to the question that you think is the most thought provoking.

Ideas and Illustrations

Below you will find a street scene with four houses missing. Complete these houses remembering only to follow the street's lines of perspective. The houses could blend in with those already drawn or be completely different. Feel free to add additional ideas to the picture. When your picture is colored, design a short story about the street, a particular person or one of the houses. Add a little creative spice to your story. Don't make it just ordinary. Attach your short story to your completed picture.

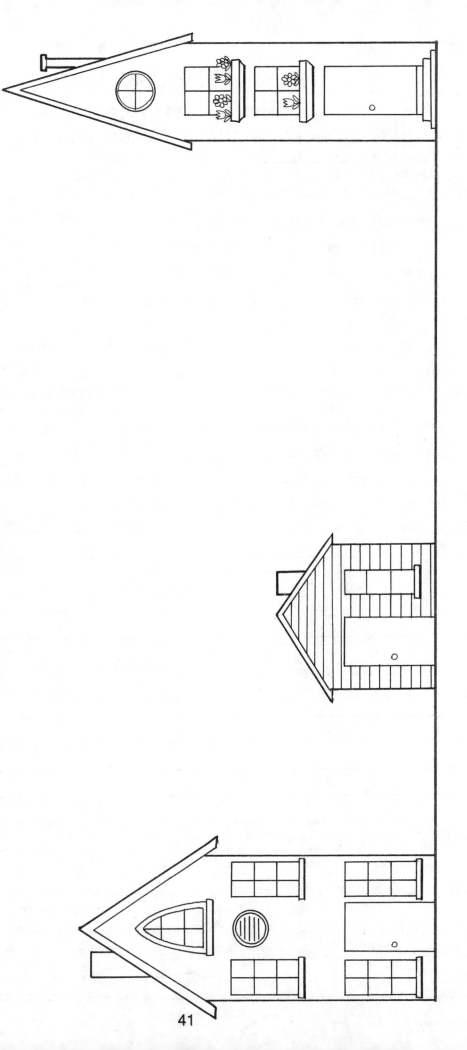

GA1152

Exaggeration Pen Pals
Short-Term Project

Judy Blume incorporates letter writing in many of her books. This inventive writing technique allows the lead character an additional vehicle to express thoughts and feelings. Review this process in *Tiger Eyes, Iggie's House* and her other writings before beginning this activity. You are going to write a letter to a pen pal. Instead of being yourself, you will write this letter as:

1. a character in one of Judy Blume's books or

2. a character from one of your favorite books or

3. a famous person in movies, TV or politics or

4. a famous explorer looking for company on your next trek

Try to pick someone who could use a friend and express why we need friends.

Author's Note: Three of the most creative character exaggerations were Godzilla, who couldn't help stepping on things, and if you would be his friend, he would invite you over to his house for a barbecue; Priscilla Presley, who tried to stop Elvis from taking drugs and was in the hospital with a broken toe and could use a friend; and Amelia Earhart who was tired of taking solo flights and was looking for someone to travel to Africa with her.

_____

_____

_____

_____

_____

_____

_____

_____

_____

_____

_____

_____

_____

_____

After writing your first draft in the space above, have your work checked before copying your letter on regular stationery. Make sure you include the pen pal information sheet with your letter. Ask the person you are writing to respond as an imaginary or real-life character, also.

GA1152

Pen Pal Information Form
Short-Term Project

This form will accompany your exaggeration pen pal letters. It will give the person you are writing information about who you really are. It will also identify your imaginary person with similar information.

Real Information

Name _____ Birth date _____ Age _____

School _____ Grade _____

School address _____

Date letter was sent _____

Person letter was sent to _____ School _____

Imaginary Information

Name _____ Birth date _____ To _____

Occupation _____

Accomplishments _____

_____

_____

_____

This letter is in response to a letter from_____

_____

_____

_____

GA1152

Creative Signing
Short-Term Project

Winnie's Beware—Private sign and the No Girls Allowed in Pool Without Bathing Caps sign are two representations of a multi-million dollar industry. The sign creation and painting industry is everywhere. Advertising companies are continually looking for people with creative ideas. What kind of ideas do you have for signs that kids would buy for their rooms? Plan your best four below and then put them on larger paper. Use the back of this paper to plan four signs that you would see outdoors. Try to make two of them humorous. Chipmunk Crossing is an example of this technique.

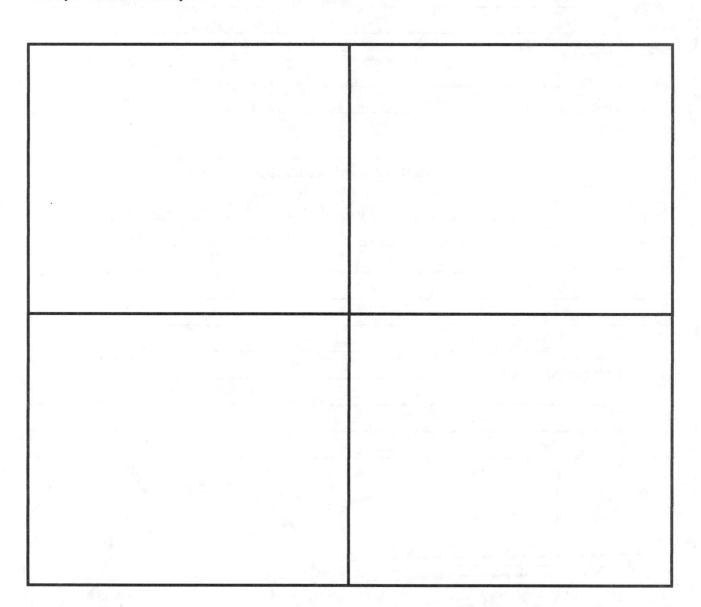

Make a portfolio of pictures of creative signs. What would a top ten list of your favorite creative signs in your area include?

Map Baseball Challenge
Drills for Skills

Materials: United States map
                    template
                    ruler

Players: opposing teams or individuals

How to Play: Each player predicts in miles the distance between the locations below. The closest prediction wins that inning. The player that wins the most innings wins the game.

Innings	Predictions	
	Player 1	**Player 2**
1. Philadelphia to Louisville	_____	_____
2. Las Vegas to Dallas	_____	_____
3. Miami to Nassau	_____	_____
4. Memphis to Nashville	_____	_____
5. Helena to Duluth	_____	_____
6. Los Angeles to San Francisco	_____	_____
7. Spokane to Boise	_____	_____
8. Winnipeg to Montreal	_____	_____
9. Yuma to NW tip of California	_____	_____

Actual Distance	Winner's Initials
1. _____	_____
2. _____	_____
3. _____	_____
4. _____	_____
5. _____	_____
6. _____	_____
7. _____	_____
8. _____	_____
9. _____	_____

Record the state or province of each of the seventeen cities on the reverse side of this page.

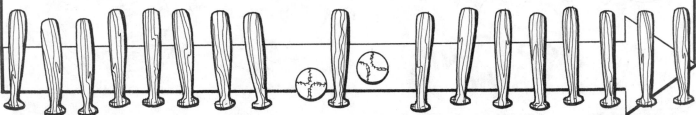

45

GA1152

Research Suggestions

Iggie's House introduces many ideas that would be good short-term projects or research initiators. Here are a few that you might undertake or incorporate as part of your literature or reading program. Hopefully one of the wide variety of ideas below will interest you or your working team.

1. Most new students feel very uncomfortable their first few days in a new school. Try to organize a new student welcome wagon and orientation club in your school or classroom. Before entering their new room, students and their parents might be given a mini program by other students in the same grade. What additional suggestions would you make for such a program?

2. Research local, national and worldwide riots. Are there any similarities or warning signs that might help you devise steps to prevent riots or quickly end them once they start?

3. Make believe you can't swim. Design ten humorous excuses for not going swimming.

4. Cut out pictures of ten dogs. Name them. Assume you are a vet and give the reason each dog is in your care.

5. What kind of agencies does your community have that would be considered minority support groups? Do they have speakers that talk to classroom groups? Highlight the activities that one of these groups performs for minorities.

6. What do you know about the sale of real estate? Invite a real estate agent to your class for such a presentation.

7. Design a What Makes a Good Friend poster.

8. Bring in the package and ad campaign for a new product for animals.

9. Make a collage of pictures of houses.

10. Research facts about Japanese customs. You can receive great information on any country by writing to that country in care of the United Nations.

GA1152

Teacher Suggestions

1. Research the dress and customs of Japan. Have the class write haiku and tonka.

2. Take a look into the differences between our educational system and that of Japan.

3. Discuss the cultural and educational wealth that can be derived from living in a multi-cultural, multi-ethnic neighborhood.

4. Talk about the educational and recreational benefits of card playing. Does playing cards make you a better thinker and problem solver? What thinking skills are involved in card playing? What card games are played most often by children? Adults?

5. Discuss the history of the exploration of Africa? Show the modernization and development patterns of the new emerging nations.

6. Research the flags of various countries. This always leads to a colorful art project as the class reproduces flags of the countries they explored.

7. Dress Up in the Garb of Your Favorite Country Day is always a big hit. Clothes, props and songs all are appropriate representations.

8. Show *The Cat in the Hat* video to your class. Introduce some words from other languages across the world for hats, coats, dogs, etc.

9. Explore the organizations in your community that assist minorities in housing, education and health services. Local organizations such as these are well prepared to give presentations to classroom students.

10. Research the different breeds of dogs and compare them to the English sheep dog.

11. The Tell Me What Science Series found at your local video store covers a great many topics found in this book.

12. Research what a poll is and how polls are used to predict public opinion.

13. Develop questionnaires with your class on five student-generated questions.

GA1152

Otherwise Known as Sheila the Great

Dog Phobia

Vacation

Swimming Lessons

Model Airplanes

White Lies

Tarrytown

Fear of Spiders

Lead-Ins to Literature

Who is Sheila Tubman, alias Sheila the Great? From the title you might think she was a magician, a queen/ruler like Alexander the Great, a braggart or just a person that was good at everything. What you might find out is that she is probably like most of us, who try to be good at something but just fall short on every attempt. Maybe she'll find out that friends that only want to be with people who are good at things can't be depended on in a pinch, or maybe she'll learn to accept everyone no matter what their personalities or faults might be.

1. What were your first thoughts about the title *Otherwise Known as Sheila the Great* and what the book might include?

   _____

   _____

   _____

2. Draw a sketch of what Sheila the Great might look like. Include pictures of five things you think she is great in doing. Use a separate sheet of paper for your drawing. List her five great aspects below.

   _____

   _____

   _____

3. This story takes place during summer vacation. In what location would you have placed the lead character and her family? Why?

   _____

   _____

   _____

4. Phobias are fears. Before reading the story, predict three fears that Sheila might have.

   _____

   _____

   _____

5. You are a phobia doctor for people afraid of ice cream. Write your analysis for one of your patients. Emphasize how he became afraid of ice cream and your steps for eliminating this fear.

   _____

   _____

   _____

6. List the steps a swimming instructor might use to teach a beginner to swim. Draw a swimming pool scene titled "First Swim."

   _____

   _____

   _____

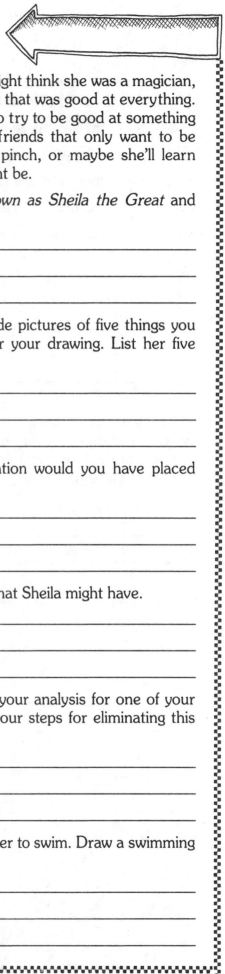

GA1152

Vexing Vocabulary I

Unscramble the italicized words to find facts from *Otherwise Known as Sheila the Great*. Write the word to the right of each sentence.

1. Sheila's mom said that she is *realclig* to trees. _____

2. *Thygie greedes* will stop you from catching pneumonia. _____

3. Ichabod Crane definitely saw the *Shelades Hamsnore*. _____

4. Sheila printed *nswe ated* across the top of the paper. _____

5. A person really good at something could be called *blarkmaree*. _____

Write three sentences where every word is scrambled. Include facts from the story. Exchange your sentences with a neighbor. Unscramble each other's sentences.

1. _____

2. _____

3. _____

Try to write three sentences where every word is in alphabetical order. Use facts from the story. An example would be: **A B**oy **C**alled **M**arty **S**ank **S**heila. Each sentence must have at least six words in it. Compete with your classmates as to who can write the longest sentence in words or letters.

1. _____

2. _____

3. _____

List the names of five swimming strokes or five types of dives normally used at your swimming areas.

1. _____

2. _____

3. _____

4. _____

5. _____

50

GA1152

Vexing Vocabulary II

equivalent
disappointed
allergic
bikini
stencil
definite
Cyrus
Washington Irving

elevator
Tarrytown
ugly
cartwheels
practical
hives
forehead
agreed

leotard
imperial
salami
haunting
flopped
breathe
absolutely
slumber

Copy each vocabulary word to the left of the twenty-four lines below. Follow your teacher's directions as he/she instructs you to write a sentence of your own using each word. The author prefers that the student find the actual sentence in the story where each word appears. This is cumbersome, at first, but necessary for realizing what relationship the vocabulary word has to the story. It also beats writing the word three times, then writing it in a sentence, then writing it in a paragraph for review. After completing this activity, turn to the back vocabulary section of the book where you will find forty-eight creative ways to follow up this assignment. Pick two activities that are challenging to you and complete them on a separate sheet of paper.

1. _____
2. _____
3. _____
4. _____
5. _____
6. _____
7. _____
8. _____
9. _____
10. _____
11. _____
12. _____
13. _____
14. _____
15. _____
16. _____
17. _____
18. _____
19. _____
20. _____
21. _____
22. _____
23. _____
24. _____

GA1152

Just the Facts

1. What floor did Sheila live on?_____

2. Where did Sheila expect to go on vacation? _____

3. What does Sheila's father do for a living?_____

4. Can you name at least four things that Sheila fears?

   _____

5. Where is Tarrytown located?_____

6. Sheila never heard of what author?_____

7. What was the favorite camp activity of Mouse, Russ and Sam? _____

8. What was "Babar Strikes Again"?_____

9. What size were Sheila's hives?_____

10. The girls composed a slam book. What is it? What were some of the categories that they used? _____

    _____

11. How would you describe the Van Arden twins? _____

    _____

12. What two pieces made up the swimming test? _____

    _____

GA1152

What's Your Opinion?

1. What is your opinion about apartment living? Can you list three advantages and three disadvantages of having an apartment?

_____

_____

_____

_____

_____

2. Just because dogs frighten Sheila, is it necessary to treat everyone that owns a dog as an outcast? Explain. _____

_____

3. Are swimming lessons necessary for people living in large cities, especially when there are few swimming opportunities available?_____

4. Do you think it is right that Sheila pretends (lies) about her ability in so many areas? _____

_____

5. What are Marty's and Mouse's best traits? Who do you think would make the better friend?

_____

_____

6. Should people prepare for things before they happen or should they adopt Sheila's policy about worrying about it when the time comes?_____

_____

7. Why do you think so many people are interested in building models? What models do you think have the biggest building audience? Check with a local store after expressing your opinion. _____

_____

_____

8. Did you find Sheila's battle with the unseen model builder funny? What is a nemesis?

_____

_____

_____

GA1152

Ideas and Illustrations I

One setting in *Otherwise Known as Sheila the Great* was the swimming area. Below you will find a kidney-shaped swimming area. Design the features of this area. Please include some of the ideas from the story before you let your creative mind add new features to the area. After you design the pool area, make a 3-D model of your design. Try adding a play area to your 3-D model.

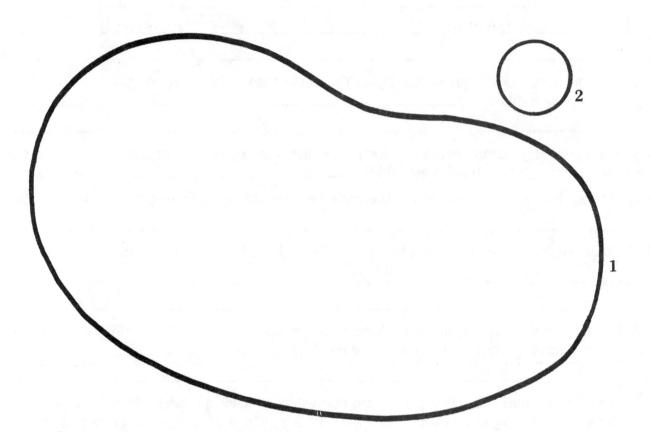

3

Draw the clubhouse here.

Number your features in the index below.

1. pool _____
2. Jacuzzi _____
3. clubhouse _____
4. _____
5. _____
6. _____
7. _____
8. _____
9. _____
10. _____

54

Ideas and Illustrations II

We discussed in Lead-Ins to Literature the things that Sheila might have been great in doing. Select four pictures of something you predicted was an area of excellence for Sheila. Cut each picture in half and paste it in the boxes below. Complete the second half of the picture with colored pencils or crayons. Draw the second half as close as possible to the original.

Greatness I	**Greatness II**
Greatness III	**Greatness IV**

GA1152

Reading Record—Short-Term Project I
Children's Literature Laboratory Data Sheet

1. What is the title of your book?_____

   _____

2. Who is the author? _____

3. Is your book a story, poem, cartoon, fact or fiction? _____

4. What is your book's library card number?_____

5. Record five important words from the story.

   a. _____

   b. _____

   c. _____

   d. _____

   e. _____

6. Give a brief summary of this work._____

   _____

   _____

   _____

   _____

   _____

   _____

   _____

   _____

   _____

7. Practice your best handwriting by copying the first and last sentence of your book in the space below. _____

   _____

   _____

   _____

   _____

   _____

   _____

   _____

   _____

8. To whom would you recommend this story? _____

   _____

Short-Term Project II
Bookmark Contest

The object of this assignment is to create a bookmark and slogan that will attract readers to good literature and to the library. Your bookmark will be judged in the following areas:

1. Creativity _____
2. Slogan _____
3. Artwork _____
4. Lettering _____

Bookmark

Make three types of bookmarks. Use this shape to practice your ideas.

1. Humorous
2. Serious
3. Space library

Experiment with other shapes for your bookmark.

GA1152

Buy or Sell
Drills for Skills

The words *buy* or *sell* can be found in each answer below. They appear in their spelling order, but the letters might not be consecutive in the final answer. After finding the answer, determine your score by putting the new letters you added over the word's total letters.

Clue	Answer	Score
Example: a school subject	**spell**ing	4/8

1. baby rabbit _____

2. grow larger _____

3. place underground_____

4. channel marker _____

5. turtle's house _____

6. pushes people around_____

7. odor _____

8. like a bee_____

9. American _____ rose_____

10. a wood finish_____

11. *Black* _____ (book title) _____

12. space/great performance _____

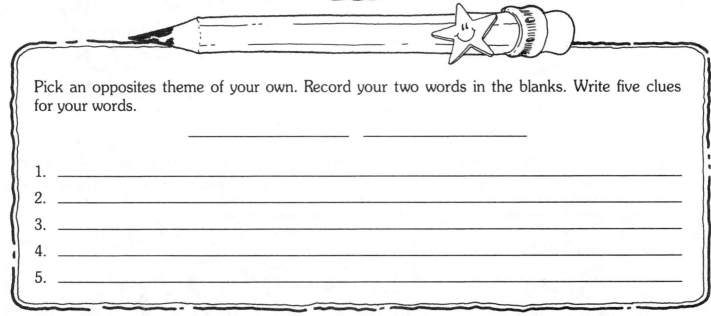

Pick an opposites theme of your own. Record your two words in the blanks. Write five clues for your words.

_____   _____

1. _____

2. _____

3. _____

4. _____

5. _____

Research

Name _____ Date _____

Famous Warriors of Fact and Fiction

Famous Warriors of Fact and Fiction focuses on those people who have battled for their countries or human rights. You are to research two people in the fact area and two people in the fiction area of this topic. Your information should contain your sources and illustrations, graphs or charts.

Some suggested topics might involve research about:

Joan of Arc
King Arthur
Hannibal
U.S. Grant
Susan B. Anthony
Gulliver
Albert John Luthuli
Mary Bethune

Harriet Tubman
Sherlock Holmes
Robert E. Lee
Anthony Wayne
Billie Jean King
Molly Pitcher
Agatha Christie/Miss Marple
Paul Laurence Dunbar

The four people I am researching are

1. _____
2. _____
3. _____
4. _____

My resources of information were

1. _____
2. _____
3. _____
4. _____

GA1152

Research—Warriors of Fact and Fiction

The paper below has been divided into two sections with two boxes in each section. The left-hand boxes should highlight your two fictional warriors while the right will house your two of fact. After using this paper for planning, teacher and peer input, finish your colorful and creative project on 11" x 14" paper. Remember to divide it into four sections after placing your title on it.

Fictional	**Factual**
Name	**Name**
Name	**Name**

60

Teacher Suggestions

1. Research with your students the number of book characters, products, sayings and people who are characterized by having the words *great* or *super* in their names.

Products	Characters	Sayings	Real People
Superglue	Superman	Super-Duper	Alexander the Great

2. Discuss with the class the people behind the scenes that you never see or hear about that help people to become great.

3. Invite a CPR team to your classroom to focus on things young people should know about CPR, helping themselves and other people in periods of medical difficulty.

4. Research your state and local laws about being a lifeguard. Follow this up with community laws for swimming pool maintenance and safety. Have your class enroll in a Red Cross life-saving and swimming program at your local pool.

5. The model making industry is quite extensive. What can you find out with your class about its size and scope? What jobs in this industry would be attractive to young children? Does anyone in the community build boats in a bottle? Have them come in to help your class build things in a bottle as part of your art program.

6. Talk with your class about famous tall tales of the past and present. Review the art of exaggeration with your class. Then, like a Mark Twain event, organize "the best liar contest." Encourage each member of your class to write one of his best tall tales and best lies for class presentation. Students may bring in three props to support their tall tales or lies.

7. Bring in some pictures by Degas and other artists showing the picture of the ballet that they are trying to present. Have two classmates wear their ballet costumes as the class tries to draw each person. Place ballet slippers on a table and have your class draw them as a still life. Follow this with a discussion of the themes of some famous ballets (*Nutcracker* to *Swan Lake*). Have your class read *Maggie Adams, Dancer.* Bring a male and female ballet dancer to class to discuss their training and work regimen.

8. Have a class yo-yo contest. Thanks to the Smothers Brothers show, there has been a national yo-yo revival. Call the Duncan Yo-Yo Company and see if one of their demonstration group's tours is close to your town. Invite them to present at an assembly.

Then Again, Maybe I Won't

Shoplifting

Rags to Riches

Five Bathrooms

Jersey City

Lisa

Basketball

Psychologist

Long Island

62

GA1152

Lead-Ins to Literature

The Tony Miglione story is truly the rags to riches life that many of us hope for. One minute he and six of his relatives are sharing one bathroom. The next minute, due to the success of one of his father's inventions, he is living in a fancy mansion. Most of us think that becoming rich doesn't present many problems. Reading *Then Again Maybe I Won't* might change your point of view. Having money certainly changed Tony or did it?

1. What are some things that a lead character might or might not do in a rags to riches story?

_____

_____

_____

2. How might a person change if he/she went from poverty to wealth? What would be the good changes? The bad changes?_____

_____

_____

3. Where would you live if you could afford any of the following locations: the city, suburbs, farm, country, island, exotic location or other? Why?_____

_____

_____

4. How might things have changed for you in each of these areas? Explain.

Friends _____

Family _____

Home_____

School _____

5. Do you think the lead character is going to enjoy the change that money brings or do you think he wants things to go back to the way they were before he moved from Jersey City to Long Island?_____

_____

_____

6. Find out how far Jersey City is from where you live. Make believe you have to travel there by bus. Chart your trip and the three places you'd stop along the way. _____

_____

_____

7. Chart your trip by air from your hometown to an exotic location. Plan three stops and describe each location's features and sites. _____

_____

_____

Vexing Vocabulary

complained	coincidence	individual
figured	electrician	emergency
president	treatment	automatically
pajamas	larynx	moustache
route	furious	binoculars
cousin	Athena	adorable
shoplifting	handlebars	responsible
fumbling	intention	detention

Copy each vocabulary word to the left of the twenty-four lines below. Follow your teacher's directions as he/she instructs you to write a sentence of your own using each word. The author prefers that the student find the actual sentence in the story where each word appears. This is cumbersome, at first, but necessary for realizing what relationship the vocabulary word has to the story. It also beats writing the word three times, then writing it in a sentence, then writing it in a paragraph for review. After completing this activity, turn to the back vocabulary section of the book where you will find forty-eight creative ways to follow up this assignment. Pick two activities that are challenging to you and complete them on a separate sheet of paper.

1. _____
2. _____
3. _____
4. _____
5. _____
6. _____
7. _____
8. _____
9. _____
10. _____
11. _____
12. _____
13. _____
14. _____
15. _____
16. _____
17. _____
18. _____
19. _____
20. _____
21. _____
22. _____
23. _____
24. _____

GA1152

Just the Facts—True and False

Evaluate each statement. Place the correct answer (true or false) next to each sentence. Write the correct answer to each false statement on the back of this paper.

1. Tony delivered the *Jersey News* to his neighbors. _____

2. Grandma's swollen larynx prevents her from speaking. _____

3. Father Pissaro's best customer is Angie. _____

4. Tony read *Great Basketball Heroes of Our Times*. _____

5. Roughage caused Tony's stomach pains. _____

6. Rosemont was Pop's dream come true. _____

7. Four new bathrooms were enough for the Miglione family. _____

8. On August 5th, Tony celebrated his thirteenth birthday. _____

9. Denton F. Buchanan was Joel's best friend. _____

10. Dr. Fogel knew about the problem of Joel's stealing. _____

Select a partner. Each of you should write five true and five false questions of your own. Combine them into a ten-question quiz. Exchange them with another team. Enter in friendly competition. See which team gets the most correct answers. Exchange questions with another team.

1. _____
2. _____
3. _____
4. _____
5. _____
6. _____
7. _____
8. _____
9. _____
10. _____

What Is Your Opinion?

1. Should Tony have said something to Joel the first time he saw him stealing?_____
_____

2. If you lost your larynx, would you learn to talk with a voice box or would you refuse like Grandma?_____
_____

3. Would you change to a job that paid more money, even though there was another job you liked more but would pay you less for performing?_____
_____

4. Was Tony's new house impressive? What was least impressive about it? Most? What features would you have added to the house? _____
_____

5. Should Tony have asked his parents the questions he had about sex? Explain. _____
_____

6. Should Maxine have been given complete control of the kitchen? Explain. _____
_____

7. Did you expect the Miglione family to change much after their move to Rosemont? Explain.
_____
_____

8. Did the author solve all the lead characters' problems by the end of the story? Do you like stories that have final endings, or do you prefer to be left hanging at the end?
_____
_____

9. Who was the most significant minor character? Explain._____
_____

10. Did Tony's doctor help him? Would you recommend a psychologist for children having noticeable problems? Would they be helpful to children without noticeable problems? How?
_____

Ideas and Illustrations

Time lapse pictures are those pictures a camera takes every thirty seconds. The camera does not move from the spot where it is focused. You, therefore, can see what changes happen over a short or long period of time. Time lapse drawing also follows this concept. Below you will find five pictures each followed by three empty frames. You are to show in your drawings how the picture will change over a short or long period of time. List the time period under each picture you draw.

Keep in mind that the camera is not moving.

GA1152

The "Extra Nice Day" Club
Short-Term Project

Many of Judy Blume's characters go out of their way to make people feel good about themselves. As a tribute to these characters, our school literature club formed the Extra Nice Day (END) club. It is dedicated to the fight to end teasing and picking on people. It also focuses on each of our attempts to make people have a happier, nicer day. Some people just don't know how to be nice. So it is each of our responsibilities to make niceness a learning process. It is our hope that each class that uses this book forms an END club. Membership is simple. First, you have to design an END button. It should contain the Extra Nice Day motto and your additional thoughts and illustrations. Secondly, you will in one week's time make five extra nice day contacts. You will record the five people you made feel extra special and indicate how you accomplished this task. You can even tell people that you are trying to join the END club and ask them how you might make their day nicer or easier. Both activities will be recorded on the pages and spaces that follow.

Extra Nice Day Successes

Person's Name	What END Task You Performed

1. _____

_____

_____

2. _____

_____

_____

3. _____

_____

_____

4. _____

_____

_____

5. _____

_____

_____

...END CLUB...

GA1152

END Button and Bumper Sticker

Each member of the Extra Nice Day (END) club is required to design an END button and bumper sticker before starting his first assignment. The Extra Nice Day slogan should be clearly displayed on each item. Both items should be eye-catching and colorful. Creatively add additional slogans and features. Discuss with your classmates how Joel and Tony's membership in such a club could have stopped the prank phone calls. Maybe it could have even stopped Joel's stealing. Are there any other characters from your favorite stories who could have also profited by being a working club member?

Button

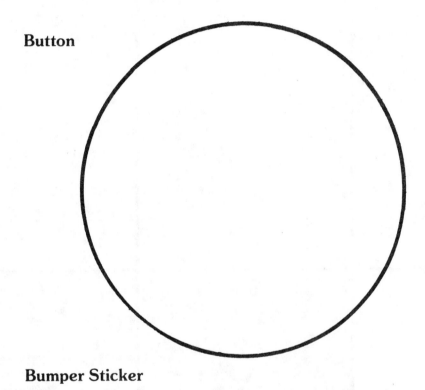

Bumper Sticker

END Club Song

The Extra Nice Day organization needs a club song, poem, flag, banner and catchy motto to use as it starts on its good deed quest. Your advertising firm has been hired to design the necessary items needed to begin the club's new membership drive. Use the boxes below for your inspiring ideas. What additional techniques does your firm recommend? How many ideas in each category will you be submitting? If you only submit one and we don't like it, do we have the right to cancel your contract?

Flag	Motto	Poem
Banner	**Song**	**Other**

GA1152

Compound Word Intersections
Drills for Skills

The following activity will help you to form compound words and will help you become a critical thinker.

1. Find each intersection.
2. Look up each letter value in the intersection.
3. Multiply each value to determine the worth of each word you created.

A-2	E-10	I-7	M-4	Q-1	U-9	Y-7
B-4	F-1	J-9	N-6	R-3	V-11	Z-8
C-6	G-3	K-11	O-8	S-5	W-13	
D-8	H-5	L-2	P-10	T-7	X-15	

11 8
1. B R E A K D O W N = 88

2. O V E [ ] O A T =

3. S E [ ] A W =

4. A N [ ] O D Y =

5. E V E R [ ] N E =

6. H O U S [ ] L Y =

7. P R I N [ ] U T =

8. B O O [ ] A S E =

9. I C [ ] R E A M =

10. B O D [ ] A S T =

11. M [ ] E L F =

O [ ] A R T =

B O [ ] I E =

B O [ ] O O D =

I [ ] O M E =

S U [ ] U R N =

B R E A [ ] O X =

T E [ ] P O O N =

B A T [ ] O O M =

P L A C [ ] A T =

H E A [ ] E S T =

P L A [ ] E N =

GA1152

Research Suggestions

1. Divide a large piece of paper into four sections. Place the title "Vision Enhancing Devices" across the top. Research four of these devices or additional thoughts of your own: binoculars, telescope, bifocals, contact lenses (extended wear or throwaways), microscopes, see-in-the-dark optics, magnifying glasses, X-ray photography or cameras.

2. Research the ten most frequently picked names for babies now and ten years ago. What percent of the names appear on both lists?

3. Pick ten of your classmates' first names and research their origins or meanings.

4. What five common birds can be found in your area? What three less frequently found birds are native to your locale? Is there an Audubon Society chapter in your area? What type of activities do they plan? Recruit a member to speak to your class.

5. Swimming pools are constructed with many types of different materials. Draw and label pictures of four different styles.

6. Electrical inventions play an important part in this story. What four designs of new inventions can you share with us? Diagram the four most recent inventions that you feel have the most profound influence on the way we now live.

7. The pen is a very common device. What is the origin of the pen and what new modifications have been made since its inception?

8. There has been a great deal of research completed in recent years on twins. Can you highlight some facts you found about similar and dissimilar circumstances that have occurred? Create a poster entitled "The Biology of Twins." Explain the difference in the various types of twins, paternal, fraternal, etc.

9. What kind of techniques are used in local stores and national chains to combat shoplifting? How big a problem, moneywise, is shoplifting to store owners? What devices would you design to combat this problem?

10. What penalties are imposed on shoplifters as compared to other types of theft? What is theft of service? Would you consider it just as severe as shoplifting? Give five examples of theft of service.

GA1152

Teacher Suggestions

1. The Bell Telephone Company has a giant film library and a wealth of kits about the telephone. Invite a speaker from your local phone company to address the class. Phone frauds, prank callers, creative systems and new inventions could be just some of the topics. New Jersey is testing a new system that allows you to see the number of the person calling you. If the lady that Joel was bothering had this device as part of her phone, she could have reported him immediately. They also are testing a "block" system. This system allows you to block certain numbers from calling your home. Big hospitals are already using a new system that allows you to see the person on the other end of your conversation. Seminars and meetings can be conducted in this fashion.

2. Discuss your area's health services with the class. Have someone come in to talk about careers in the health service field. There are hundreds of jobs and talents needed in addition to doctors and nurses.

3. Team your class up with the residents of a local old age home for shared teaching and tutoring. The Philadelphia school system has a program called RSVP Retired Senior's Volunteer Program which brings hundreds of retired citizens into schools and classrooms for one-to-one teaching. Write for information on what is an easy program to start anywhere.

4. Is there a local gamblers, alcoholic or theft organization in your area that has prevention and help programs for school age children?

5. Have the class research songs that have to do with friendship.

6. Have the class research the things Long Island Is Long and Short On or What's New in New Jersey?

7. Research the voice and larynx with your class. The PBS program *In Search of a Voice*, new inventions and medical breakthroughs of the eyes, ears, nose and throat are three challenging directions for study.

8. Good Apple's *Everyday Law for Young Citizens* is an excellent resource in allowing children to understand the law as it pops up through character misdeeds (Joel's shoplifting) in the literature they read.

9. Research with your class the process of patenting or claiming work on a new invention, idea or scientific principle.

73

Freckle Juice

Secret Potions

Self-Worth

Foolish Beliefs

Freckle Counting

Magic Marker Dots

74

GA1152

Lead-Ins to Literature

Why in the world would anyone want freckles? Andrew thinks that everyone should have freckles on the back of the neck. Andrew thinks that if you have freckles on the back of your neck, your mother will never be able to tell whether you washed it or not. *Freckle Juice* is the story of Andrew's quest to get freckles. He wants them so much that he even invests his money in a freckle juice formula that guarantees him freckles.

1. Do you think this formula will really grow freckles on Andrew's face and neck?

2. What type of fun do you think Andrew's classmates will have with Andrew when they find out he is looking for a secret freckle formula?

3. Who would you first see if you wanted to have freckles? Would you discuss it with your parents before drinking any cure-all formulas or juices?

4. What percentage of the people in your class have freckles or birthmarks?

5. If you were to sell a magic freckle formula, would you put it in a juice, a liquid, a shot or a cream?

6. Do you think that after Andrew's magic formula gives him freckles that other children will want to know his secret for freckle success?

7. Do you think Andrew is an older person or a younger person? Could an adult be fooled by a special formula that will remove or restore any facial features?

8. If you were trying to fool Andrew, would you tell him that the magic potion would take effect immediately, overnight or in a few days?

9. Do you think the classroom teacher will inform Andrew on how silly it is to request a secret freckle formula?

GA1152

What Is Your Opinion?

1. Who was the more humorous character—Andrew or Sharon? _____

_____

2. If you could make a magic formula that could restore or remove something, what would it be? _____

_____

3. Do you think a goal of never having to wash is a good one? _____

_____

4. Do you think daydreaming is important for people to do? _____

_____

5. Do you think oral reading in front of everyone in your classroom is necessary to become a good reader? _____

_____

6. How much would you have charged for a freckle juice recipe? _____

_____

7. Sharon's secret recipe for freckle juice was handed to Freddie on a piece of paper. Do you think that is an appropriate way to keep something secret? What features would you have added to the letter to keep the formula a secret? _____

_____

8. Do you think it was right for Andrew to be banned from using the oven and the stove?

_____

_____

9. What other things do you feel that children are forbidden to do without any real justification?

_____

_____

10. How do you feel about Miss Kelly coming to Andrew's rescue? _____

_____

11. Do you think Sharon will ever leave well enough alone and save her other classmates from her secret formulas and pranks? _____

_____

12. How many things can you name that smell and are still good for you? _____

_____

13. What secret hiding places would you recommend on a person's body, in a bedroom or in the classroom? _____

_____

14. What did you think of Andrew's magic marker solution to stop kids from teasing him?

_____

_____

GA1152

Vexing Vocabulary

arithmetic   attention   recipe
mumbled   whispered   scratched
tissue   zipper   stuffed
aisle   mayonnaise   vinegar
panted   alongside   formula
wrapped   package   dropout
appendicitis   Marcus   stomach
vegetable   blur   pretended

Copy each vocabulary word to the left of the twenty-four lines below. Follow your teacher's directions as he/she instructs you to write a sentence of your own using each word. The author prefers that the student find the actual sentence in the story where each word appears. This is cumbersome, at first, but necessary for realizing what relationship the vocabulary word has to the story. It also beats writing the word three times, then writing it in a sentence, then writing it in a paragraph for review. After completing this activity, turn to the back vocabulary section of the book where you will find forty-eight creative ways to follow up this assignment. Pick two activities that are challenging to you and complete them on a separate sheet of paper.

1. _____
2. _____
3. _____
4. _____
5. _____
6. _____
7. _____
8. _____
9. _____
10. _____
11. _____
12. _____
13. _____
14. _____
15. _____
16. _____
17. _____
18. _____
19. _____
20. _____
21. _____
22. _____
23. _____
24. _____

GA1152

Vexing Vocabulary—Student Generated

One of the hardest jobs a teacher has is teaching his/her students to make their own decisions on what is important to study. Instead of studying things you already know, this work sheet will give you a chance to generate words that you don't know. Words that you think are special or words that you would like to remember should also be recorded below.

What two words would you pick from *Freckle Juice* to study in each of the following categories?

1. Person's name _____   _____

2. A place _____   _____

3. A noun_____   _____

4. An adjective _____   _____

5. A compound word_____   _____

6. A scientific word _____   _____

7. A foreign word or word generated from another language _____   _____

8. A well-written phrase_____

_____

9. A hard-to-spell word _____   _____

10. A commonly confused word _____   _____

Select ten words from the story that would add to your writing skills. Use them in a short description of what you will be doing ten years from now.

_____   _____   _____   _____   _____

_____   _____   _____   _____   _____

Age ten years from now _____   Story Title _____

_____

_____

_____

_____

_____

_____

    GA1152

The Creative
Writing Chart
Drills for Skills

A. "I don't know what to write about" cries from students can be eliminated by the development of a creative writing chart with each student. The categories are flexible and are designed to always have a wide range of ideas in front of the undecided writer. The chart can be completed in school or at home and kept in a writing journal or sustained silent writing book.

B. Students complete the chart below with their favorite topics in:

Books/ Movies	Things I'm Interested in Knowing	Places I'd Like to Visit	Sports/ Hobbies	Way Out Ideas	Family Facts

GA1152

Mystery Madness
Short-Term Project

Mysteries, creatures and stories of the occult have had a strange fascination over the years.

A. What are the unique characteristics of these stories?

_____
_____
_____
_____
_____
_____
_____
_____

B. Why do you think they have such a universal and historical appeal?

_____
_____
_____
_____
_____

After completing the questions above, color in the character the way you think he'd look after drinking freckle juice.

80

GA1152

Ideas and Illustrations

Each box below is designed to hold your best creative and magical secret formulas. Take your time before you devise the secret formulas for the following:

Freckle Juice	Love	Kindness	Health

Friendship	A Pet	Sunshine	Travel

Draw a picture of the making of a secret formula. Be sure to include pictures of yourself and the formula's secret ingredients.

GA1152

Research Suggestions

1. There are many products that have mixed ingredients. Fold a paper into four sections. In column one, write down five products. In column two, make a prediction of three of the products' ingredients. Column three will contain the list of actual ingredients. Draw a picture of the product in column four. Peel the labels from some of the most commonly used products. Investigate one of the ingredients. Does it have any potential dangers? What is the function of your local consumer protection agency? How would you register a product complaint with the agency?

2. What are the major brands of juices sold at your local food stores? Find out what percentage of your class uses each brand. What percentage of actual juice does it contain? What does *made from concentrate* mean?

3. There are many types of containers for liquids that are used in your local stores. Find out which ones are environment friendly. Does your community have a recycling program? How does it operate compared to other locations? Michigan gives ten cents for each returned container. What does your area do?

4. Design a medical explanation of Freckles' poster. Some additional topics to choose from might include measles, acne, moles, warts, hives, chicken pox and birthmarks. Yuck!

5. *The Peanut Butter Solution* is very similar to *Freckle Juice*. What common denominators can you find in both stories?

6. What nonprescription medical solutions are used the most in your area? Brainstorm with your team or classmates how you might research this question.

7. Make a "boy do I get advice from all over the place" survey showing one week's worth of advice. Include the type of advice, the person who gave it to you and the total amount of advice received during a week. Separate the advice into a good advice and bad advice section of your survey.

8. What are the ingredients for invisible ink? Set up an invisible ink letter writing project. Compose letters that famous people would have sent in secret. Detail who it is being sent to and why.

9. Make a "problems that need to be solved" presentation.

10. Keep track of how many problems your teacher has to try to solve in a week's time. Could you have suggested alternative soutions to any of them?

82

Superfudge

Advertising Agency

The Art Gallery

Art History

Turtle the Dog

N.Y.U.

Spider-Man

Lead-Ins to Literature

Superfudge sounds like a story that is going to take place in a candy store or on the boardwalk at some beach. If you have read *Tales of a Fourth Grade Nothing*, you will soon realize it is Peter Hatcher again with a whole set of new problems. Not only is his brother Farley the world's biggest pain in the neck, but his mother is expecting another baby. This should put him still further down on the list of ever getting respect or attention from his parents.

1. What cute things do you think Fudge will comment about in this story?

   _____

   _____

2. Predict from your own experience five ways that younger brothers and sisters can drive you crazy?

   a. _____

   b. _____

   c. _____

   d. _____

   e. _____

3. What three things do young children do that parents say "Oh, don't worry. He's only a baby"?

   a. _____

   b. _____

   c. _____

4. Joanne, who hardly ever talks to Peter, comments on how adorable Fudge is. This bothers Peter. Can you name three other things that people do or say to you when you are caring for a younger child?

   a. _____

   b. _____

   c. _____

5. Fudge learns how to ride a bike in the story. Predict some of the catastrophes that he has riding his bike to school.

   _____

   _____

6. Peter is fooled by a morning wake-me-up call from Fudge. What do you think happened?

   _____

   _____

7. Peter gets upset when his mom hugs Fudge. What type of situation would cause this to happen?

8. The family is planning a move from New York City to Princeton, New Jersey. What problems will this cause for Peter Hatcher?

   _____

GA1152

Vexing Vocabulary
Student Generated

One of the hardest jobs a teacher has is teaching his/her students to make their own decisions on what is important to study. Instead of studying things you already know, this work sheet will give you a chance to generate words that you don't know. Words that you think are special or words that you would like to remember should also be recorded below.

What two words would you pick from *Superfudge* to study in each of the following categories?

1. Person's name _____ _____

2. A place _____ _____

3. A noun_____ _____

4. An adjective _____ _____

5. A compound word_____ _____

6. A scientific word _____ _____

7. A foreign word or word generated from another language

   _____ _____

8. A well-written phrase_____

   _____

9. A hard-to-spell word _____ _____

10. A commonly confused word _____ _____

Select ten words from the story that would add to your writing skills. Use them in a short description. You are a doctor who is discussing a child's poor relationship with his/her parents due to a younger sibling.

_____ _____ _____ _____ _____

_____ _____ _____ _____ _____

Job title_____ Story title_____

_____

_____

_____

_____

_____

_____

DECISION

GA1152

Vexing Vocabulary

cultured
whack
tousled
metropolitan
privileges
Princeton
nursery
actual

fortified
Sesame Street
pregnant
museum
charge
university
crystal
botch

catastrophes
gravy
somersaults
Roxanne
suspense
wound
vitamins
daughter

Copy each vocabulary word to the left of the twenty-four lines below. Follow your teacher's directions as he/she instructs you to write a sentence of your own using each word. The author prefers that the student find the actual sentence in the story where each word appears. This is cumbersome at first, but necessary for realizing what relationship the vocabulary word has to the story. It also beats writing the word three times, then writing it in a sentence, then writing it in a paragraph for review. After completing this activity, turn to the back vocabulary section of the book, where you will find forty-eight creative ways to follow up this assignment. Pick two activities that are challenging to you and complete them on a separate sheet of paper.

1. _____
2. _____
3. _____
4. _____
5. _____
6. _____
7. _____
8. _____
9. _____
10. _____
11. _____
12. _____
13. _____
14. _____
15. _____
16. _____
17. _____
18. _____
19. _____
20. _____
21. _____
22. _____
23. _____
24. _____

Just the Facts

The vocabulary word on the left must be used as you generate a fact from the story. Each word can be found in *Superfudge*. Incorporate the word in your fact.

1. certificate

   _____

   _____

2. naughty

   _____

   _____

3. commercial

   _____

   _____

4. fortified

   _____

   _____

5. Kreskin's crystal

   _____

   _____

6. advertising history

   _____

   _____

7. coincidence

   _____

   _____

8. bonjour

   _____

   _____

9. annoyed

   _____

   _____

10. commuting

   _____

   _____

11. contagious

   _____

   _____

Write facts that compare Tootsie to Fudge, Grandma to Peter, Daniel to Fudge, Turtle to Uncle Feather.

What Is Your Opinion?

1. Farley Drexel Hatcher, better known as Fudge, must have some good points! Can you highlight three of them?

   a. _____

   b. _____

   c. _____

2. Do you think Peter has a right to be fed up with all the antics that Fudge has pulled in this story?

   _____

3. Do you think Fudge is still cute and adorable, or do you think Judy Blume crossed over that line in the things she had him say and do in this new story?

   _____

   _____

4. What options did Peter have open to him to stop from seemingly always being upset at the things Fudge has done?

   _____

   _____

5. Did any of the minor characters stick out in your mind as major contributors to the story?

   _____

6. Three children proved quite a load for Peter's mom. Grandma came over to help ease the burden. What is the difference between caring for two or three children?

   _____

   _____

7. The Hatcher family hardly ever seems to go out. Do you think this would make life a little happier for them if they got out more?

   _____

   _____

8. Mom wants to go back to college to study art history. Where will she find the time to do this and care for her family?

   _____

   _____

9. Daniel gives a great lecture on birds. Would you consider him an exceptional child?

   _____

   _____

10. Joanne and Peter seem to like each other. How will this relationship be developed in future stories? Did you enjoy their interaction in this story?

    _____

    _____

11. Did Peter overextend himself in his request letter to Santa?

    _____

Protest

How can I show them
When they say I must
That I don't want to?

Why can't they see
That I just can't
And what's more shan't?

How can I tell them
That what they want
I do not?

I cannot
So I say
Okay.

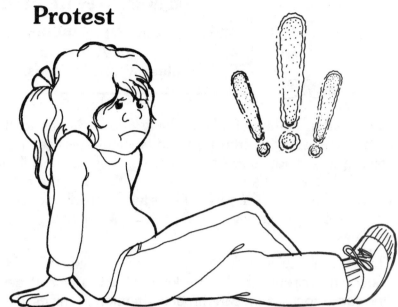

A. Felice Holman wrote this unique poem about a person in a mental dilemma. From the poem, can you describe the person's characteristics and explain the problem as you and the author see it?

_____

_____

_____

_____

B. What are three things you might protest? What are some ways people use to protest things they are dissatisfied with? Can you design a unique protest and the steps you would take to organize it?

_____

_____

_____

_____

C. Design three placards that Peter Hatcher could carry to protest Fudge—moving to Princeton, being ignored by his parents, against cute kids. What would you place on the cards if you were Peter?

_____

_____

_____

_____

GA1152

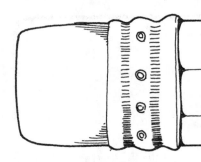

Short-Term Project

Spectacles
by Ann Beattie
Illustrations by Winslow Pels

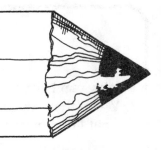

Ann Beattie, author of *The Burning Bed*, switches to this children's tale of the unexplained, as magic spectacles transport the leading character back in time. There, the lead character tries to find if adults are correct when they continually tell her that "things were better back when." The author's poetic style of writing and the delicate illustrations of Winslow Pels help weave a *Through the Looking Glass* tale of childhood. Just like Alice in her journey, the heroine, because of her journey to the past, is better able to handle the critical adult world in which she lives.

This journal review introduces a character like Peter Hatcher in *Superfudge*. Peter wants to know why parents think little kids are so cute and deserving of so much parent attention. *Spectacles* focuses on parent/adult attention to things in the past.

After reading *Superfudge*, write a character sketch for the girl in *Spectacles*. Before writing the sketch, list things that you might want to include as part of her appearance, personality, interests and attributes. Take some of Peter Hatcher's character traits and see if any of them would be of suitable help in building this new person.

Building a Character Sketch Note Boxes

Appearance	Personality	Interests	Attributes

Use the information in the boxes above to now write your character sketch below.

_____

_____

_____

_____

_____

_____

_____

_____

GA1152

Stained Glass
Short-Term Project

The story *Spectacles* talks about seeing the world quite differently when looking through special glasses. You are to design a stained glass window. Below the window create in your own words the special view your window gives you of the world.

Window Sketch

The Story You See Looking Through Your Window

What view of a better relationship with Fudge and the baby might Peter have seen?

Word Ladder Creative Speller for Partners or Teams
Drills for Skills

Your spelling ability and your ability to select information that is not common will be tested in this challenge. You will be given words of various sizes. You will try to use the letters in the given word to create other words of six, five, four, three, two and one letter. You will score one point for each word that is not duplicated on any of your group's papers. You may only use letters the same number of times they appear in the original word. A blank sheet follows for your own creative speller creations. Challenge your classmates with them.

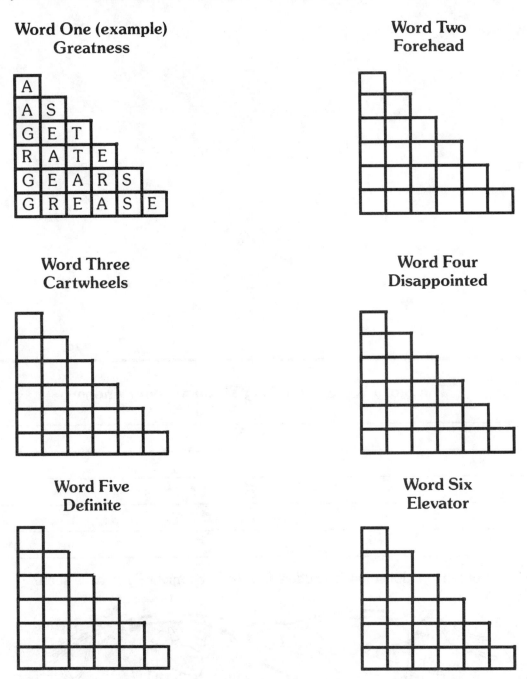

Word One (example)
Greatness

A					
A	S				
G	E	T			
R	A	T	E		
G	E	A	R	S	
G	R	E	A	S	E

Word Two
Forehead

Word Three
Cartwheels

Word Four
Disappointed

Word Five
Definite

Word Six
Elevator

Student Hint: Remember you are trying to select words that no one else has.

Word Ladder Creative Speller for Partners or Teams
Drills for Skills—Blank Master

Your spelling ability and your ability to select information that is not common will be tested in this challenge. You will be given words of various sizes. You will try to use the letters in the given word to create other words of six, five, four, three, two and one letter. You will score one point for each word that is not duplicated on any of your group's papers. You may only use letters the same number of times they appear in the original word.

Word One

Word Two

Word Three

Word Four

Word Five

Word Six

GA1152

Superfudge Research
Literature Find Out Form

This form was designed so you can share some of your thoughts about literature with new friends.

What is your favorite book?_____

Who is your favorite author?_____

Who is your favorite poet?_____

1. Find someone who dislikes your favorite book. Find out why.

   _____

2. Find someone who likes chocolate. _____

3. Can you find a person who has read three books by the same author?

   _____

4. Find someone who plays a musical instrument. _____

5. See if someone believes in both ESP and UFO's._____

6. Find someone who has fallen asleep reading. _____

7. Who has recently attended a play? _____

8. Find someone who has read the book and seen the movie, filmstrips, video or play.

   _____

9. Find someone who doesn't have a library card. _____

10. Find two people who read more than they watch TV. _____

11. Does anyone have twins in his/her family? _____

12. Can you find someone who knows what foreshadowing is? _____

13. Find someone who keeps a diary or journal._____

14. Find someone who likes cold weather._____

15. Can you find someone who can identify five characters from Greek or Roman mythology?

   _____

   _____

Friends interviewed_____

New people interviewed_____

Total in class _____

Percent of class surveyed _____

One, Two, Three

The numbers 1, 2 or 3 play an important part in literature and in each problem below. The class may use their 1, 2, 3 giant cards or write the answers on the appropriate blanks.

Example: Little Pigs ___3___ , Hydrogen Composition in Water ___2___

A. "These were the best of times" _____

B. Terms Washington served _____

C. Billy Goats Gruff _____

D. Pigs that went to market _____

E. Even prime _____

F. Impeached Presidents _____

G. Cinderella's stepsisters _____

H. World wars _____

I. Island continents _____

J. Equal sides of an isosceles triangle _____

K. Suns in our solar system _____

L. Syllables in *funny, beauty,* etc. _____

M. _____ Company

N. _____ Gentlemen from Verona

O. _____ Nations Under God

P. Female super heroine _____

Q. For the money _____

R. A homonym _____

Can you write some one, two, three clues that would challenge us in literature areas that we should know? Record as many book titles as you can think of that have numbers in the title *The Twelve Seasons*, etc.

_____
_____
_____
_____
_____
_____
_____
_____

Tiger Eyes

Teddy Bear

Wolf

Los Alamos

Overprotective Relatives

Death of a Father

Quiet Walks

Welcome to New Mexico

Atlantic City

Nuclear Energy

Lead-Ins to Literature

Davey Wexler's father has just been killed in a holdup at his 7-Eleven store. The trauma is tearing at Davey, her mother and younger brother. Friends try to help, but little can be done to ease the family's pain. The family moves temporarily from Atlantic City to Los Alamos, New Mexico. The new environment seems to add extra problems. Somehow, slow solutions start to take root. New friends begin to help. Another death of someone close to her helps Davey to see her fears a little more clearly.

1. Death, illness, divorce, sex and family problems are difficult subjects to have to discuss after a literature reading. What agencies in your school, church, town and state are set up to supply teenagers with support in these areas?

   _____

   _____

2. How might a story like this help someone that might someday have the same or similar problems?

   _____

   _____

3. Should the school be a forum for such problems? Should it be left to the home or church?

   _____

   _____

4. What kind of literature is available in your school on such topics as death, suicide, divorce, drug use and family problems?

   _____

   _____

5. There are many types of problems where running away might be the answer. There are other problems that cannot be solved by running away. Evaluate this statement and give two examples of each situation.

   _____

   _____

6. You often hear that a change of scenery might do you some good. Does this apply to moving, or can you stay where you are to accomplish a new outcome? Explain.

   _____

   _____

7. What type of crime statistics are available in your community? How would you use these statistics to combat crime and alert people to possible dangers without scaring them? Do you have a Neighborhood Watch program in your area? How does it operate?

   _____

   _____

 GA1152

Vexing Vocabulary

Los Alamos
diamond
achievement
Sinai
Big Sur
pamphlets
embarrasses
whisks

ironic
sprawling
fabricated
audience
security
balmy
hostile
Adidas

portraits
parched
scrubby
Oklahoma
Charlotte
monitor
detonated
suede

Copy each vocabulary word to the left of the twenty-four lines below. Follow your teacher's directions as he/she instructs you to write a sentence of your own using each word. The author prefers that the student find the actual sentence in the story where each word appears. This is cumbersome at first, but necessary for realizing what relationship the vocabulary word has to the story. It also beats writing the word three times, then writing it in a sentence, then writing it in a paragraph for review. After completing this activity, turn to the back vocabulary section of the book, where you will find forty-eight creative ways to follow up this assignment. Pick two activities that are challenging to you and complete them on a separate sheet of paper.

1. _____
2. _____
3. _____
4. _____
5. _____
6. _____
7. _____
8. _____
9. _____
10. _____
11. _____
12. _____
13. _____
14. _____
15. _____
16. _____
17. _____
18. _____
19. _____
20. _____
21. _____
22. _____
23. _____
24. _____

GA1152

Just the Facts

1. In what part of the body was Davey Wexler's dad shot? _____

2. How old is Jason Wexler? _____

3. After her father's death, what does Davey have concealed under her pillow? _____

4. After Davey faints in school, what does the nurse think she has? _____

5. Dr. Foster says that _____ made her hyperventilate and pass out.

6. What was the code name for the building of the atomic bomb? _____

7. What caused Jason's nosebleed at the table? _____

8. What does Davey buy on Wolf's advice? _____

9. Who has been waiting for Davey in the hospital? _____

10. In what state does Wolf attend school? _____

11. What reason does Davey give for the large number of churches in Los Alamos? _____

12. What does Wolf's dad call Davey? _____

13. What does *cuando los lagartijos corren* mean? _____

14. Davey isn't allowed to take what subject in school? _____

15. What did Wolf's father leave Davey? _____

16. What was the nickname of Davey's mother's date? _____

17. What play did Jane promise to try out for? _____

18. What did Jason make for Valentine's Day? _____

19. What did Walter have caught in between his teeth at the dinner table? _____

20. Where did "A Woman Without a Man Is Like a Fish Without a Bicycle" appear?

_____

GA1152

What Is Your Opinion?

1. Did it surprise you that the story started with a murder and funeral? Explain.

   _____

   _____

2. How many books have you read whose theme was that of a parent's death?

   _____

3. Why weren't Davey and Jason any comfort to their mother?_____

   _____

4. Did you think staying in bed was the answer to Davey's problems after the funeral?

   _____

5. What types of things would you have done to prepare someone for the first-day-in-high-school panic? _____

   _____

6. Did you think that two weeks in Albuquerque would be enough to resolve Davey's and her mother's problems? _____

   _____

7. Do you think that the United States should have built and used the atomic bomb?

   _____

8. Would you recommend canyon exploring to city slickers from New Jersey?

   _____

9. Do you think you would qualify for a search and rescue squad?

   _____

10. The city of Los Alamos was proud of its development of the atomic bomb. Give your opinion of this statement.

    _____

    _____

11. How do you think President Truman felt about dropping the bomb on Japan?

    _____

12. What kind of comfort did Wolf provide Davey and his Father?

    _____

13. Did you feel that Davey could have treated Walter, Ned and Bitsy better?

    _____

14. Under the circumstances do you think everyone was overprotective of Davey?

    _____

15. Why do you think Wolf sent Davey the Tiger Eye without leaving any return address or way to contact him?

    _____

16. There's a saying that says "There is no place like home." Do you think this is true?

    _____

17. What did you think of the author's cover illustration on this book? Is it representative of someone who had sad or "Tiger Eyes"?

    _____

GA1152

Ideas and Illustrations

You will find, after researching American Indian art, that it has few equals in the area of design and fashion. Below you will find four areas for your reproductions of a floor mosaic, necklace and medallion, bracelet, hat, dress, blanket, pottery, realistic painting or another representative of Indian art that you may have discovered.

Indian Art Contributions

Jewelry	Home
Fashion	**Art**

Collage Poetry
Short-Term Project

Most students are familiar with the steps in developing a collage. Pictures depicting one theme are cut out of many different sources and placed in a boundary. This boundary is usually the size of the picture or form that you'd like to make. Collage poetry follows a similar guideline. You are to pick a theme (say the ocean). You will then find eight different poems that have lines that parallel your theme. From each poem you will pick one line. When you are finished you will have an eight-line poem from eight different sources. Your poem need not rhyme, but if you choose a rhyme scheme, the task is infinitely more challenging.

Poem title _____ Poem theme _____

Lines

1. _____

2. _____

3. _____

4. _____

5. _____

6. _____

7. _____

8. _____

Source

1. _____

2. _____

3. _____

4. _____

5. _____

6. _____

7. _____

8. _____

GA1152

I'll Take It, You Take It
Teacher Directions

Over one hundred years ago, Lewis Carroll invented the word chain. It was called doublets and involved starting from the word *head* and arriving at the word *foot*. The rules were simple. Each word below the previous word can only change by one letter. The letter order may not be changed. You can go from *head* to *herd*, but not from *head* to *hand*. The person, years ago, who arrived at the final word in the least amount of moves was declared the winner. The TV program *Chain Reaction* uses word chains that go from first to last, but in their case the word that follows just has to be related in some way to the word above it. They even allow rhyming words and opposites. Rhyming words and opposites are not allowed in the game below.

Pass out the score sheet on the following page. Place the big-to-pocket grid that is in the box on the chalkboard. Divide the room into two teams. Explain to the class that the word under *big* is related to it. The same is true for the word over *pocket*. They have to determine what word follows or is before each of them. Select a team to go first. Before they guess a word they may ask for a letter. For instance, "I'll take a letter under *big*." They could have also asked for a letter over *pocket*. The teacher then puts a *B* under *big*. Hands raised. Anyone on that team can take a guess at what they think the word is. If they miss, the other team controls. You get only one guess each time a letter is given. If the other team then asks for a letter under big, they would have an *E* added to the *B* and would see *BE* on the board. They can now guess. The last letter of a word can never be given. A blank is placed there, *BE* indicating to the selecting team that you can't place a letter there before they guess, because it is the last letter. The team that guesses the word correctly controls the board. They then can select where they would like the next letter.

Another option for the control team is to say to the teacher that they would like to give a letter to the other team under or over a certain word. In doing this they hope that after giving a letter to the other team, the other team still won't be able to solve it. Control would then come back to the original team, and they would see one more letter added to the word before they would have to make their guess. This, of course, could backfire if the team you gave the letter to makes a good guess and gets the word. The team that determines the last word is the winner. The other team could get five words, but if you get the last word, you are the winner.

GA1152

I'll Take It, You Take It

Drills for Skills

Score Sheet

Big	Bills	Open
_____	_____	_____
_____	_____	_____
_____	_____	_____
_____	_____	_____
_____	_____	_____
_____	_____	_____
Pocket	Keys	Hearted

Team	Tall	Glad
_____	_____	_____
_____	_____	_____
_____	_____	_____
_____	_____	_____
_____	_____	_____
_____	_____	_____
Possess	Rug	Bars

Newspaper	Cheese	Mountain
_____	_____	_____
_____	_____	_____
_____	_____	_____
_____	_____	_____
_____	_____	_____
Expert	Meadow	Rocket

GA1152

I'll Take It, You Take It

Drills for Skills

Answers

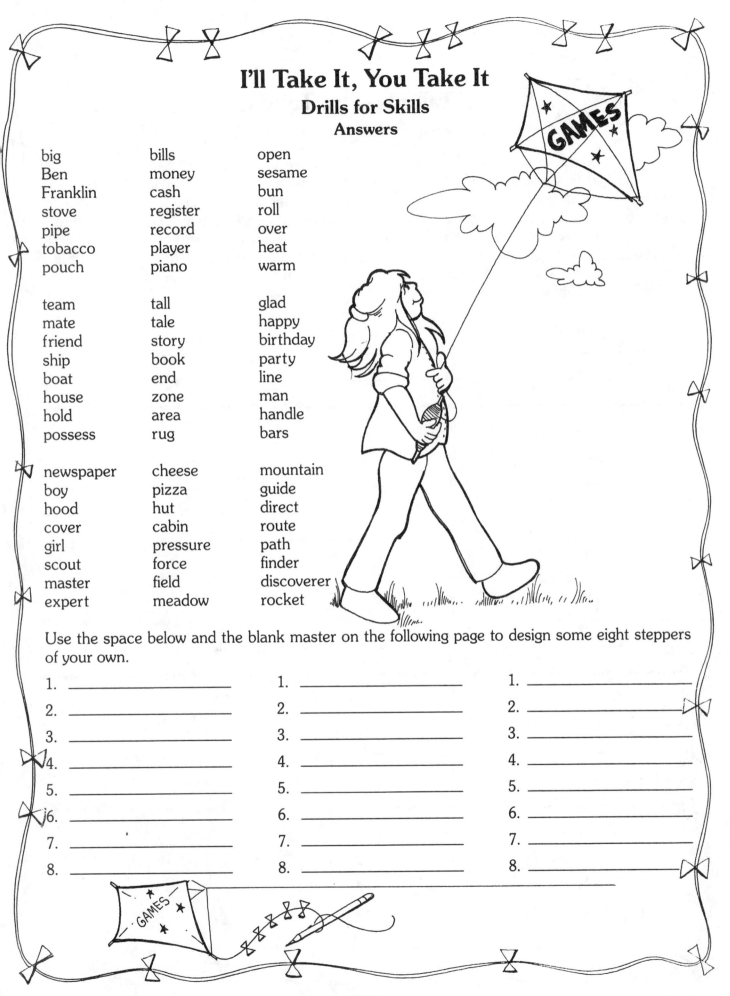

big	bills	open
Ben	money	sesame
Franklin	cash	bun
stove	register	roll
pipe	record	over
tobacco	player	heat
pouch	piano	warm
team	tall	glad
mate	tale	happy
friend	story	birthday
ship	book	party
boat	end	line
house	zone	man
hold	area	handle
possess	rug	bars
newspaper	cheese	mountain
boy	pizza	guide
hood	hut	direct
cover	cabin	route
girl	pressure	path
scout	force	finder
master	field	discoverer
expert	meadow	rocket

Use the space below and the blank master on the following page to design some eight steppers of your own.

1. _____   1. _____   1. _____
2. _____   2. _____   2. _____
3. _____   3. _____   3. _____
4. _____   4. _____   4. _____
5. _____   5. _____   5. _____
6. _____   6. _____   6. _____
7. _____   7. _____   7. _____
8. _____   8. _____   8. _____

GA1152

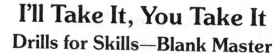

I'll Take It, You Take It
Drills for Skills—Blank Master

Keep the word chain that you have written hidden. Have your classmates use the first eight blank lines on this blank sheet to write the first and last words in your chain. You can now play the game as your teacher did or use this student version. The class still asks you for letters, but each time a letter is given you receive a point. Each time your classmates use one guess they must ask for another letter. This, of course, increases your score. If the class completes the puzzle requesting less than fifty percent of the letters, they win. If they need over fifty percent, you win. This percentage changes to twenty percent for superior classes. You can decide on a percentage before the game starts.

Game 1
1. _____
2. _____
3. _____
4. _____
5. _____
6. _____
7. _____
8. _____

Game 2
1. _____
2. _____
3. _____
4. _____
5. _____
6. _____
7. _____
8. _____

Game 3
1. _____
2. _____
3. _____
4. _____
5. _____
6. _____
7. _____
8. _____

Game 4
1. _____
2. _____
3. _____
4. _____
5. _____
6. _____
7. _____
8. _____

Game 5
1. _____
2. _____
3. _____
4. _____
5. _____
6. _____
7. _____
8. _____

Game 6
1. _____
2. _____
3. _____
4. _____
5. _____
6. _____
7. _____
8. _____

GA1152

Research Suggestions

1. Many people only think of Atlantic City as the gambling capital of the eastern seaboard. It is much more than that, both culturally and historically. Create another side to an Atlantic City poster after researching the city and surrounding areas.

2. The Southwest is rich in Indian history, law and tradition. What top ten sites would give a visitor the best appreciation of what Indian culture has contributed to American life? Briefly highlight their importance.

3. There is a very strong link between New Jersey and Los Alamos in the development of the atomic bomb. What is this link and who were the principal characters in its development?

4. Compose a poem and design a card for someone who has lost a member of his/her family?

5. The Save-Our-Ocean campaign needs new ideas. What would you suggest?

6. Design a wall painting similar to those found in the caves of the Midwest. Depict ideas from the present or imagine it repesents a past lifetime.

7. Fold a piece of art paper in half. On the left make a collage of cutout or drawn western wear. On the right do the same thing for Atlantic City wear.

8. Research the number of Miss America winners from each state in the United States. Make a unique graph depicting your findings. Try doing this in a pictograph, using the map of the United States.

9. Research property ownership at your courthouse. Invite a real estate seller or developer to come to your classroom to discuss current trends in real estate development in your area.

10. How many national and local women's organizations can you name? What are some of their goals?

11. There are many regional and national magazines that might add information to the Tiger Eyes story. Name two well-known magazines and two obscure magazines that might be sources of information that correspond to the story.

GA1152

Teacher Suggestions

1. The contrast between Atlantic City, New Jersey, and Los Alamos, New Mexico, should give impetus to many book extensions. Discuss compare and contrast strategies before encouraging discussion and research in these areas:

   a. Ocean vs. Desert
   b. Wild vs. Domestic Animals
   c. Guns vs. Gun Control
   d. Private Business vs. Corporations
   e. Nuclear vs. Antinuclear Weapons
   f. Inpatient vs. Outpatient Care
   g. Family Dependence vs. Self-Exploration and Self-Dependence

2. Investigate the advent of the atomic age. Explore the advantages and disadvantages of nuclear energy. Invite speakers into the classroom who are knowledgeable in each area and form of persuasion. Teach your class some simple rules about debate evaluation.

   a. Concentrate on the presentation of facts. Without good information you won't see things as they really are. You will see things as someone wants to make you think they are. Judgements should be made from facts.
   b. Information is a powerful tool. Read about the debate topic from a number of sources before attending a presentation. Ask speakers about their sources of information and whether they have read some of the same sources you have.
   c. Don't be swayed by good speakers with poor facts.
   d. Be ready to ask questions to clear up points that leave you uncertain.
   e. Take notes and compare your speaker's key arguments.
   f. Research some of the key points after the presentation. Half facts sometimes seem very convincing until you read the original context.

3. Develop with your class the different voices that an author can use to write a story.

   a. Writing the story as a principal or minor character
   b. Writing as an outside person viewing the happenings
   c. A man writing as a woman telling her point of view
   d. A woman writing through a male character in the story
   e. How about through the eyes of the family pet

4. Discuss the significance of folklore and oral literature with your class.

5. Discuss strategies in crisis writing. Have the class list crises that would make interesting reading/writing.

The One in the Middle Is the Green Kangaroo

Play Practice

Being Yourself

Hand-Me-Downs

Sixth Graders

Laughter   Acceptance   Audience

GA1152

Lead-Ins to Literature

Being a middle child has its good and bad points. In Freddy Dissel's second grade mind, all the points were bad ones for him. From big brother Mike to little sister Ellen, he just can't seem to win. Maybe becoming an actor would help him get over his problems. Maybe being the only second grader in the sixth grade school play would add to his problems. Surely dressing up as a green kangaroo will only make kids tease and pick on him. Then again maybe the green kangaroo comes to his rescue and saves him from being the one in the middle.

1. What do you think two good points in being a middle child might be?

    a. _____
    _____

    b. _____
    _____

2. What could be wrong with being a middle child?

    a. _____
    _____

    b. _____
    _____

3. Would you have picked the color green for a kangaroo? Why?

    _____
    _____
    _____
    _____

4. What animals would you be willing to act like in a play?

    _____ _____ _____
    _____ _____ _____

5. What troubles could baby sister cause?

    _____
    _____

6. If a play has a green kangaroo in it, what kind of play would it be?

    _____
    _____

7. How could an older brother bother his younger brother?

    _____
    _____

GA1152

Vexing Vocabulary

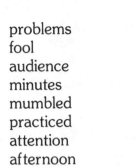

problems
fool
audience
minutes
mumbled
practiced
attention
afternoon

peanut
clothes
middle
laughed
mirror
wonderful
dinner
bow

squeezed
special
kangaroo
stomach
giggled
screamed
auditorium
pinched

Circle the correct answer that will complete each sentence below.

1. Freddy had (no, some, two, normal) problems.

2. Freddy was the (smartest, oldest, youngest, middle) child in the Dissel family.

3. After the play everyone took a (nap, break, bow, rose).

4. Before Ellen was born, Freddy used to have his own (dog, cat, room, toys, clothes).

5. Ellen screamed when Freddy (fell, kissed her, pinched her, took her doll away).

6. The great middle nothing was (Mike, Ellen, Freddy, Ms. Gumber).

7. "Break a leg" means (good luck, be careful, eat your food, take smaller bites).

8. Being the green kangaroo was (tiring, easy, silly, important).

9. What kind of a hug did Freddy get on the day of the play? (warm, caring, big, extra hard, nice)

10. Green kangaroos were in Freddy's (schoolbag, classroom, dreams, kitchen).

Write four circle-the-correct answer sentences to exchange with the members of your class. Please use facts from the "Green Kangaroo" story.

1. _____

2. _____

3. _____

4. _____

GA1152

Just the Facts

Write two factual questions that we could answer about each situation below.

1. Mike dealing with Freddy

   _____

   _____

2. Freddy playing with Ellen

   _____

   _____

3. Freddy's bad feelings about his life

   _____

   _____

4. Ms. Matson and the play

   _____

   _____

5. Mom and Dad at the play

   _____

   _____

6. The day everyone heard about the school play

   _____

   _____

7. Freddy on stage

   _____

   _____

8. Back home after the play was over

   _____

   _____

What's Your Opinion?

1. Do you think Freddy's problems were that upsetting? Explain your reasons, please.

_____

_____

2. What problems would you consider to be serious problems for Freddy?

_____

_____

3. Do you think hitting younger children is necessary to stop them from doing improper things?

_____

_____

4. Why was the role in the play so important to Freddy?

_____

_____

5. Do you think Freddy's parents loved him more before or after the play? Why?

_____

_____

6. Was the green kangaroo really an important part of the play?

_____

_____

7. Freddy did lots of training for his part in the play. Do you think most adult actors would have to train as hard as a child actor?

_____

_____

Write three of your opinions or points of view about the story in the space below.

_____

_____

_____

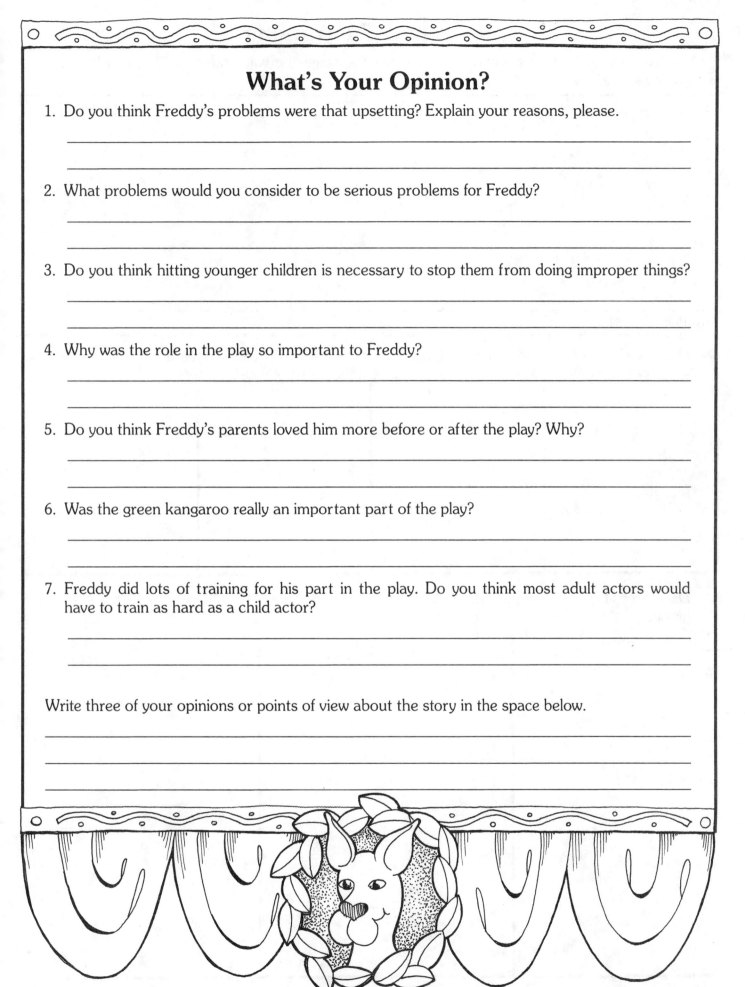

Ideas and Illustrations

The outlines of a stage appear below. Design the stage the way you think it would look for Freddy's play.

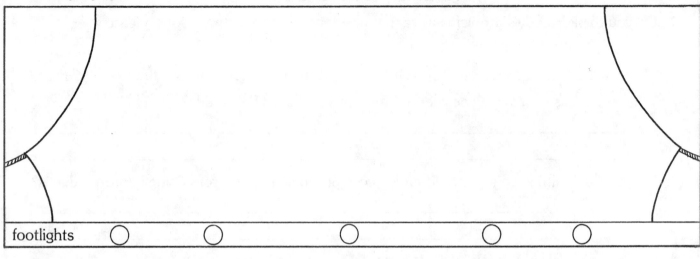

footlights

Draw the costumes of four of the characters you think might have appeared in the play. See if you can use cutout paper or material for the outfits of two of your characters.

Draw an as-I-got-older picture of Freddy. Show what he looked like in second, fourth and sixth grade.

Second   Fourth   Sixth

114

Short-Term Projects

Most people have seen fluffy beanbag chairs being used by children reading or watching TV. Animal magnets or refrigerator magnets are in millions of homes. These two ideas seem simple. Someone, though, is making a lot of money thinking about and then marketing things we all can use. You are the chairman of a company that makes kangaroo products for the home, yard, car and office. Draw your original kangaroo products for these four areas in the spaces provided below. Describe your products on the back of this paper. Two examples of products might be a toothbrush holder in the shape of a kangaroo, where you put your toothbrush in the kangaroo's pouch, or a garbage can, where you put your garbage in the kangaroo's pouch. See what you can invent.

Home	Car
Office	**Yard**

What other points from your reading gave you ideas for new and exciting products for the car, home and office?

GA1152

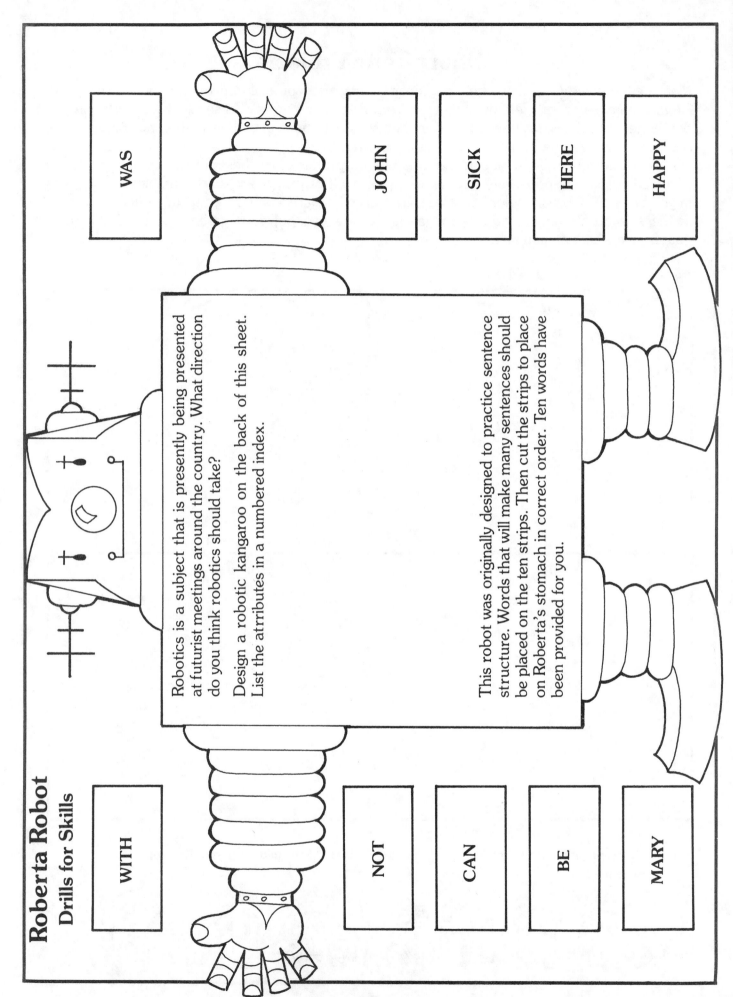

Roberta Robot
Drills for Skills

WAS

JOHN

SICK

HERE

HAPPY

WITH

NOT

CAN

BE

MARY

Robotics is a subject that is presently being presented at futurist meetings around the country. What direction do you think robotics should take?

Design a robotic kangaroo on the back of this sheet. List the attributes in a numbered index.

This robot was originally designed to practice sentence structure. Words that will make many sentences should be placed on the ten strips. Then cut the strips to place on Roberta's stomach in correct order. Ten words have been provided for you.

GA1152

Research Suggestions

Until the exploration of Australia over two hundred years ago, very few people knew what a kangaroo looked like. Today, it is the most recognized of the pouched mammals. The kangaroo comes from an order of animals called marsupialia. *Marsupialia* is derived from the word *marsupium*. In Latin, *marsupium* means "pouch." The pouch serves as sort of a developer for baby kangaroos, because at birth the baby kangaroos are not yet fully developed. The underdeveloped kangaroo jumps into the mother's pouch at birth and remains there for food and warmth. When it is developed it leaves the pouch. This usually happens when the baby is about six months old. There are tons of interesting ideas you might want to research about the kangaroo. Most of us don't live close enough to a zoo to do animal behavior studies on kangaroos or talk to zookeepers about kangaroo behavior. Yet, there are numerous periodicals where you can find information about the areas suggested below.

Use the spaces below to record notable findings.

1. What can you find out about Australian history?

2. Who first discovered the kangaroo?

3. What does Australia do to protect the kangaroo?

4. What kind of habitat does the kangaroo live in?

5. Describe the kangaroo's body features.

6. Compare the kangaroo to our opossum.

7. Were there prehistoric kangaroos? How did their size compare to today's kangaroo?

8. What distinguishes the gray kangaroo?

9. Why do red kangaroos travel in herds?

10. Does the kangaroo have any natural enemies?

11. Is the kangaroo a threat to farmers or the land that they graze on?

12. How did the kangaroo get its name?

13. What is the leaping and running ability of kangaroos compared to other animals?

14. Research other animals of the region—koala, Tasmanian devil, wombat or the tree kangaroo.

Pick two of these questions to concentrate on for your research. Please know a little about each question that you didn't go into as deeply as your two major choices.

Teacher Suggestions

The play, family interaction and the kangaroo all provide excellent pre and follow-up activities for the story.

1. Make a classroom mural titled "The Animals of Australia."

2. Make a bulletin board whose theme is the Island Continent and Other Famous Islands.

3. Make a survey board where children vote for plays that they liked best.

4. Discuss the difference between a movie and a play.

5. Take the children to a theater to examine the props and physical feature aspect of a well-equipped stage.

6. Talk about how sets and designs are made in small versions before being expanded to giant play-sized scenery and settings. Have the class make dioramas of the settings for their own imaginary plays.

7. Collect and discuss playbills and their attributes. Pick three children's plays where the class can design their own playbills. In the playbill they will use their own family, friends and pets as the leading characters.

8. Design the set for a rock video (diorama or full-size). Have the class then perform and videotape the lip synched event.

9. Discuss the good and bad points of having older and younger brothers and sisters.

10. Have each pupil design a poster for the sale of his pet kangaroo.

11. Have each child write a letter giving five reasons he should be able to keep his often naughty pet kangaroo.

12. Have each child design the best brother or sister one could possibly have. Story and index of this special person's features should be included with the drawing.

13. Bring in a baby name book and discuss the derivations and meanings of student names. Then allow the children to invent and list nice meanings of their classmates' names.

14. Have children design a kangaroo animal ride.

15. Have the class design a putt-putt golf course with Australia or animals as the theme.

GA1152

It's Not the End of the World

Aunt Ruth   Parent Problems

"C" Average Day

Lawyers

Emotions

Furniture

Divorce

Good Day Book

Getting Them Back Together

GA1152

Lead-Ins to Literature

It's Not the End of the World sounds like it involves a serious topic—that someone is going to tell the lead character to grit her teeth and things will work themselves out. Karen Newman tries to work her parents' separation out. She seems to be in way over her head. What can she say to stop them from fighting and being mean to each other? It gets so bad that her diary has marks in it for and against the parent that started the most recent fight. When her dad moves out, she still tries to get them to talk with each other. A runaway brother doesn't help nor does blaming herself for the separation. Maybe in time they will work things out. In the meantime, her day book still has more bad days in it than good.

1. Would there be anything that someone could say to someone to ease the pain of her parents' impending divorce? _____

2. Do you think divorce affects girls more than boys? _____

3. Why do you think recording her thoughts each day in a day book could be helpful and give Karen a better understanding of her life and her problems? _____

4. Should Karen's parents have discussed their separation with the kids before her father moved out of the house? _____

5. Do you think pets are a comfort to people going through family difficulties? _____

6. Do you think everyone should have access to the boys' and girls' book about divorce? _____

7. Should the same thing be available to teenagers concerning other important topics? _____

8. What do you expect to learn from Karen Newman's difficulties. _____

9. Do you think the problems concerning divorce presented in a book could help a person in similar situations? _____

10. Do you think that children should decide on visitation rights during a divorce settlement? _____

11. What would you do if someone became hysterical in front of you? _____

12. Why do you think the courts generally give custody of the children to the mother in a divorce case? _____

120

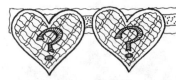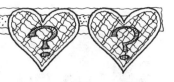

What Is Your Opinion?

You have been asked to generate a survey of the five questions that are most on young readers' minds after completing *It's Not the End of the World*. What do you think those five questions would be? Can you write your point of view and what you think the opposite point of view would be for the five questions?

1. Yours _____

   Opposite _____

2. Yours _____

   Opposite _____

3. Yours _____

   Opposite _____

4. Yours _____

   Opposite _____

5. Yours _____

   Opposite _____

6. Do you think anyone could have helped Karen Newman with her problems?

   _____

   _____

7. Books like this are supposed to help you realize that you are not the only one in the world that has such a problem. What other function does a story like this serve?

   _____

   _____

8. Karen's brother comes home under a no-questions-asked policy. In what other circumstances is this policy used? Where else would you recommend its use?

   _____

   _____

9. Some people work through their problems by helping others. What would you suggest Karen do in the area of self-help through helping others?

   _____

   _____

10. How do the problems of parents affect the way children think? Karen says she will never get married. Surely this statement comes from observing her parents' marriage.

    _____

    _____

 GA1152

Vexing Vocabulary
Student Generated

One of the hardest jobs a teacher has is teaching his/her students to make their own decisions on what is important to study. Instead of studying things you already know, this work sheet will give you a chance to generate words that you don't know. Words that you think are special or words that you would like to remember should also be recorded below.

What two words would you pick from *It's Not the End of the World* to study in each of the following categories?

1. Person's name _____ _____

2. A place _____ _____

3. A noun _____ _____

4. An adjective _____ _____

5. A compound word _____ _____

6. A scientific word _____ _____

7. A foreign word or word generated from another language_____ _____

8. A well-written phrase _____

   _____

9. A hard-to-spell word _____ _____

10. A commonly confused word_____ _____

Select ten words from the story that would add to your writing skills. You are a TV host of a program called *It's Not the End of the World*. Use the ten words in your description of the program.

_____ _____ _____ _____ _____

_____ _____ _____ _____ _____

Job title _____ Story title _____

_____

_____

_____

_____

_____

_____

_____

Make Your Own Decisions

GA1152

Vexing Vocabulary

miserable	mocha	dependable
accident	Noxzema	concentrate
hollered	muscles	San Francisco
refrigerator	insurance	thermometer
sponge	initials	nonsupport
divorce	Kentucky	diorama
showcase	restaurant	conceited
sergeant	vacuum	advance

Copy each vocabulary word to the left of the twenty-four lines below. Follow your teacher's directions as he/she instructs you to write a sentence of your own using each word. The author prefers that the student find the actual sentence in the story where each word appears. This is cumbersome at first, but necessary for realizing what relationship the vocabulary word has to the story. It also beats writing the word three times, then writing it in a sentence, then writing it in a paragraph for review. After completing this activity, turn to the back vocabulary section of the book, where you will find forty-eight creative ways to follow up this assignment. Pick two activities that are challenging to you and complete them on a separate sheet of paper.

1. _____
2. _____
3. _____
4. _____
5. _____
6. _____
7. _____
8. _____
9. _____
10. _____
11. _____
12. _____
13. _____
14. _____
15. _____
16. _____
17. _____
18. _____
19. _____
20. _____
21. _____
22. _____
23. _____
24. _____

GA1152

Student Interview
Short-Term Project

The following interviews have been designed to help you build a character sketch for future story writing. Find two subjects and record their answers to these questions. Write three questions of your own that can be included in each interview.

Name of subject _____ Age _____

Grade _____ Brothers _____ Sisters _____

Like best about school _____

Like least about school _____

Like to do when home _____

Favorite TV show _____

Hobby/Collection _____

Pets _____

Name of subject _____ Age _____

Grade _____ Brothers _____ Sisters _____

Like best about school _____

Like least about school _____

Like to do when home _____

Favorite TV show _____

Hobby/Collection _____

Pets _____

Please record three questions of your own on the back of this paper. Record your subjects' answers to these questions.

GA1152

Ideas and Illustrations

The events in *It's Not the End of the World* lend themselves to a myriad of art activities. Add your ideas to the ten art ideas that are found below.

1. Make the drawings of three pictures that you would find on a calendar representing this month and the two that will follow. Add silly holidays on the dates you select for their observance.

2. Make a portfolio of modern and antique furniture. Draw an example for two of your original designs in either the modern, contemporary or antique mode.

3. Pick a piece of furniture, like a lamp, and create your creative designs for it. Please remember to state the function of each for those not as well versed as you are.

4. Design the storefront for the Global Insurance Company or Newman's Modern Furniture store.

5. Make the ground plans for an apartment building. Complete your plans using toothpicks, blocks, clay or any other material that you have available. Have a toothpick Eiffel Tower building contest with your classmates.

6. Design a poster with accompanying saying that would let kids know that no matter how much it hurts, it is not the end of the world when something traumatic happens.

7. Write a poem titled "Snowball Fight" under a snowball fight scene.

8. Design a new front for the Howard Johnson, Holiday Inn, Marriott or Days Inn hotel chain. If you feel successful, try the same thing for a fast food franchise like Burger King, McDonald's or Pizza Hut.

9. Visit an art museum or gallery in your area and critique three of the paintings.

10. Keep a sketch and doodle pad handy. Try to draw for ten minutes each day. This sounds like the sustained silent reading and writing programs that you already have in school. You will soon see the benefits of doing something on a regular basis.

GA1152

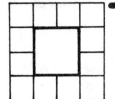
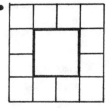

Literature Squares
Drills for Skills

Literature squares will challenge your book and short story knowledge. Each square has a four-word solution. Words one and three are written across. Words two and four are written downward. Clues for the four answers are provided. The first letter in word one is also the first letter in word two, while the last letter in word one is the starting letter for word four. You do not have to solve the clues in order. Many times doing number four or another obvious answer will help you to determine less obvious answers. Two blank pages are provided for you. The first page will be used to solve the clues below. The second page is for your creations. Hand your clues and the second page to a classmate to be completed.

A.   (6 by 6)

1. Our opposite of Hades
2. The messenger god
3. Black Beauty's home
4. Chocolate maker

B.   (6 by 6)

1. Dressed a chicken in clothes
2. Type of multicolored sock
3. Camp Counselor/Turtle on Nose
4. Another word for *illustrator*

C.   (5 by 5)

1. Samuel Clemens
2. William Blake's animal
3. Russian money
4. James Clavell's _____ House

D.   (6 by 6)

1. Alice's "behead her" queen
2. Streetcar for racing
3. The Reluctant _____
4. _____ Kellog (author and illustrator)

E.   (5 by 5)

1. Hell in Greek myths
2. Queen of Troy
3. Wrote "The Tooth Witch"
4. Francis _____ Key's banner

F.   (5 by 5)

1. Goliath's enemy
2. A friend of Snow White
3. Story with a moral
4. Steer a car

G.   (5 by 5)

1. Miss Longstockings
2. _____ the Burro
3. Miss Oyl
4. Good Night _____ (song)

GA1152

Literature Squares

Student Directions: Use this sheet to solve the clues on the previous page.

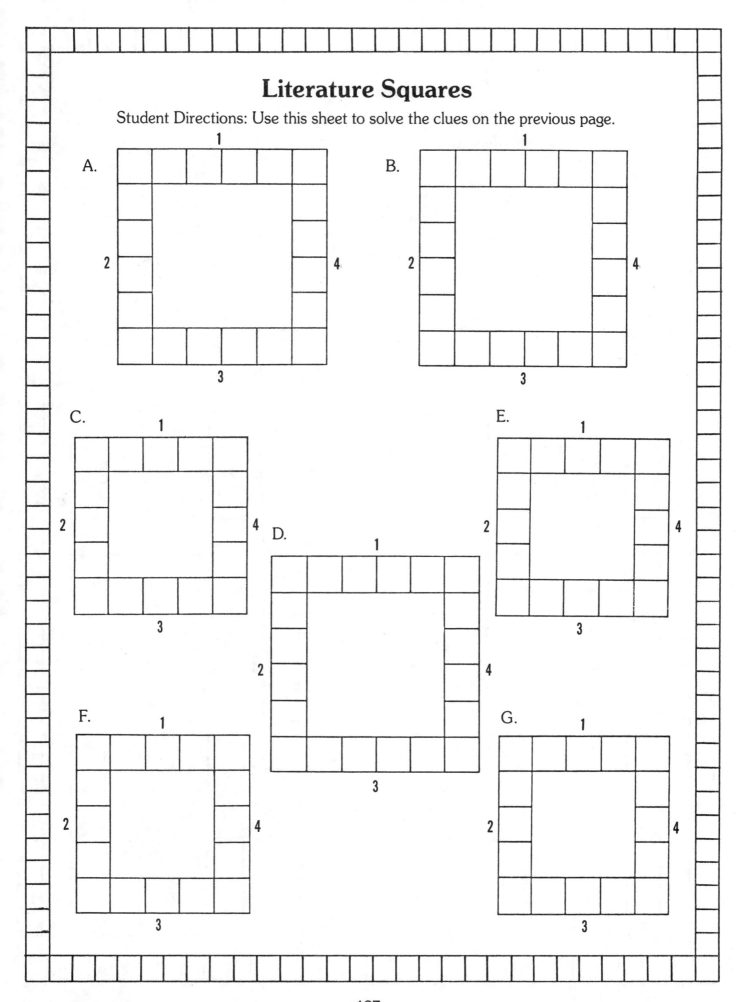

GA1152

Literature Squares
Blank Master for Student Clues/Puzzles

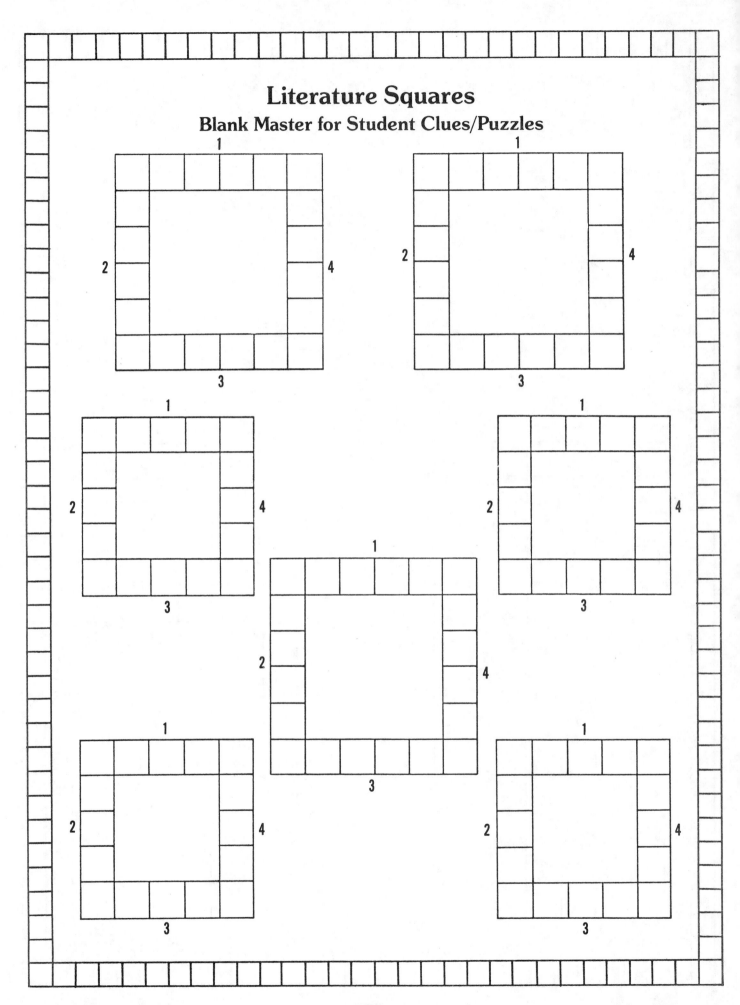

GA1152

Just As Long As We're Together

New Friends

Silly Squabbles

Go Team

The School Bus

Pajama Parties

Hunks   **Parent Help**   **Boyfriends**

GA1152

Lead-Ins to Literature

Just As Long As We're Together sounds like a story of either a child and his/her pet, a husband and wife or the feeling of a tongue stuck to the roof of a mouth too full with peanut butter. None of those three choices is the correct one. *Just As Long As We're Together* follows the escapades of three friends since childhood as they try to keep their friendship together. New friends, vacations away from each other, family problems, growing pains and silly spats are blended into the story. "Is it too much of a task to remain close or will friendship win out" seems to be the underlying theme of the story.

Place your comments after each point below.

1. Does it matter that the lead characters are girls? Could boys have the same problems? When you read, do you ever switch the sex of the book characters and say "That same thing happened or could happen to me"?
   _____

2. What types of problems and concerns make it most difficult for friends to stay friends?
   _____

3. Do you feel more comfortable with just one special friend or a group of friends?
   _____

4. Would you trust your best friend with your most personal secrets?
   _____

5. What qualities should a good friend have?
   _____

6. Should your best friend support you even when he knows you are doing something wrong to yourself and others?
   _____

7. Do you have to work at being a good friend or is it just natural to be friends with someone?
   _____

8. Where would you predict that the friends in this story had their best times together?
   _____

9. Can you catalog some stories where boys were friends; girls were friends; boys and girls were friends?
   _____

10. What themes do the designers of friendship cards focus their poems and writings on?
    _____

11. What literary character would you choose as a best friend? Why?
    _____

GA1152

Vexing Vocabulary

optimist	lecture	announcement
tendency	shrieked	Vietnamese
orthodontist	substitute	anniversary
forsythia	scratching	imitated
horror	combination	shivered
debate	Hawaii	responsibility
applauded	adjusted	depressed
revealing	generation	la creme de la creme

Complete each sentence below without moving the key vocabulary word to a different position. Each blank represents one word. You are not permitted to add any additional spaces.

1. _____ _____ depressed _____ _____.

2. Forsythia _____ _____ _____, _____ _____?

3. _____ horror _____ _____ _____.

4. _____ _____ _____ _____ responsibility.

5. Revealing _____ _____ _____.

6. _____ applauded _____ _____ _____ adjusted.

7. Optimist _____ _____!

8. _____ shrieked _____ _____ orthodontist.

Write five, five-word sentences using the word *adjusted* in each of the five possible positions. Score two points for each sentence that is a question. One point is given for all others.

1. Adjusted _____ _____ _____ _____.

2. _____ adjusted _____ _____ _____.

3. _____ _____ adjusted _____ _____.

4. _____ _____ _____ adjusted _____.

5. _____ _____ _____ _____ adjusted.

Pick two vocabulary words from the list above that you can write in the four positions of a four-word sentence.

_____

_____

_____

_____

_____

GA1152

Just the Facts

Write a false fact about each of these situations. Exchange this sheet with a friend. Have him/ her record the correct answer under your false fact. Don't make your sentences so obvious that even a person who hasn't read your story can turn the words in your false sentence around for the correct answer.

1. Stephanie and hunks

   false _____

   true _____

2. The girls concerning boys their age

   false _____

   true _____

3. Maizie's use of language

   false _____

   true _____

4. Alison's feelings about being adopted

   false _____

   true _____

5. What it feels like having a movie star for a mother

   false _____

   true _____

Change these facts to false statements.

Bruce believed that everyone should write to the President. Stephanie's letter indicated that she thought war was stupid.

The girls were called "Macbeth" because of their likeness to characters in the William Shakespeare play.

Rachel was upset that her dad was dating and not willing to spend private time with her.

Bruce went fishing with his father; he probably didn't consider it a violent act.

Talking about their problems helped Rachel and Stephanie realize their true feelings.

Rachel's bee-sting necklace could save her life. She should have worn it at all times.

Mrs. Robinson was concerned over Rachel and Stephanie's disagreement.

GA1152

What Is Your Opinion?

1. Is it possible to have two best friends that you can share all your secrets with?
   _____

2. Were the girls wrong to be jealous of new friends being included in one another's friendship groups?
   _____

3. Should parents become involved when children seem to be having relationship problems with one another?
   _____

4. Do you prefer all-school assemblies or assemblies where the young children are separated from older children's activities?
   _____

5. If you were the new teacher, would you have stopped Eric as soon as he started introducing his classmates with the special names that he has given them?
   _____

6. Do you remember the first gift you ever received from someone of the opposite sex? If you were to give a first gift, what would it be?
   _____

7. Was one of the girls more to blame for their fight and breakup? Who? Why?
   _____

8. What boy in the story played the largest role in the girls' lives?
   _____

9. If you are better than your best friend in a certain school subject, do you think it is necessary to hide this skill?
   _____

10. Too many people confess to being poor in math instead of giving the subject their best effort. Do you find this true in your school and home? Explain.
    _____

11. Do you prefer sleepovers at your own house or at the house of one of your friends?
    _____

12. What is your opinion of overnight camps versus day camps?
    _____

13. What is your favorite cookie? Have you ever encountered an incredible brownie?
    _____

14. Were Jeremy Dragon's names for people a sign of hidden creativity?
    _____

15. What was the most creative aspect that you have found in books that you have read?
    _____

GA1152

Do Your Syllables Make Sense?
Drills for Skills

1. This does not make real good sense. (all one-syllable words)

2. Monkeys carried honey into Hidden Valley. (two-syllable words)

3. Governor Benedict rewarded everyone's outstanding performance. (three-syllable words)

Can you write two one-syllable, two-syllable and three-syllable sentences below? Each sentence should have at least six words.

1. _____

1. _____

2. _____

2. _____

3. _____

3. _____

Can you write a two-syllable short story? Two-syllable words are the only words that may be used.

_____

_____

_____

_____

_____

_____

_____

GA1152

Book Review Writing and Rating
Short-Term Project

The Temptation of Wilfred Malachey
By William F. Buckley, Jr.
Illustrations by John Gurney

In his first book for the school market, William Buckley presents Wilfred Malachey: bright, poor and thrust into the elite environment of Brookfield Academy. Add a computer with its hidden Omegagod, a school curse, petty thievery, romance and a "what really happened at the end" ending and you have the ingredients of a good mystery.

John Gurney's eye-catching and well-coordinated illustrations added to the suspense. Mr. Gurney resides in Bucks County, Pennsylvania. He financed his formal art training by drawing caricatures on the Atlantic City Boardwalk.

Book rating on a scale of 1-10 (poor to excellent)
Story 7, Illustrations 8, Creative situations 8

The entry above is representative of a book review that might be found in a journal or Sunday review section of the newspaper. After reading *Just As Long As We're Together*, write a journal review and include your rating scale in the space below. Highlight your favorite book using the same format. Read William Buckley's book and write a criticism of its story and artwork. What positive comments would you add to the review above?

_____

_____

_____

_____

_____

_____

_____

_____

_____

_____

_____

_____

GA1152

Personal, Three Friends and Great Books Seal

Ideas and Illustrations

After looking at your state seal and the United States national seal, use the space below to design a personal seal representative of you, your family and interests. Each piece of your seal should be described in an index below your drawing. Then ask your librarian for books that have the Newbery and Caldecott seals on them. Using similar techniques, design your school's award seal that will be placed on outstanding books in your library. *Just As Long As We're Together* focuses on three friends. Design a three-friends seal.

Personal, Library or Three-Friends Seal

In the space below, please describe your reasons for selecting the symbols that you used in your seal.

_____

_____

GA1152

Research Suggestions

1. Make a booklet of pictures and stories of movie stars and their children.

2. Research the world's most beautiful beaches; then make a mini poster selecting your five favorite beaches as the subject.

3. Find out the theme of *Macbeth*. Are there any other stories from your readings that have similar situations?

4. Research the adoption laws of your state. Try to find out if there are different requirements demanded of state and private agencies.

5. Pick a holiday and show three countries that celebrate it differently.

6. Research a community problem and write a letter to your mayor asking for assistance and outlining some of your solutions.

7. Design a friend's T-shirt listing the attributes of a good friend.

8. Compare the two chief industries of New York with those of California.

9. Write a newspaper article about the children who had to flee Vietnam.

10. Research what three baby advice books and what three literature selections lead their respective top ten.

11. Make an acrostic poem with the letters in *Connecticut* stressing it as an ideal place to live.

12. Answer the question why New York never sleeps with supportive facts.

13. What type of food programs for the needy does your community offer? Make a booklet of their services, contact number and community projects.

14. Research the voice and imitation capability of animals.

15. Write an entry for your diary about a day at Malibu Beach.

16. Find the three most frequently purchased Mexican dishes at your local supermarket, restaurant and fast food stand.

GA1152

Teacher Suggestions

1. It is a pajama party. Write the dialogue that would be spoken by three members attending the party.

2. Write a letter to the state tourist commissions of New York, Connecticut and California with your class. Compare the response of the three locations. Have your class check the 800 number directory for the agencies and industries within each of these states that might give your class additional information.

3. Write the milk marketing board with your class and compare the milk production from each area.

4. Have your class go on an author hunt to see how many famous authors were born in California, Connecticut and New York.

5. Have your class conduct a fashion show titled "The Hats of New York, California and Connecticut."

6. Invite a speaker in from a local adoption agency to talk to your class. Have your class write a list of questions to the speaker before the speaker arrives.

7. Write book companies that your school deals with and ask them their book donation procedures and the prices for damaged books.

8. Organize a neighborhood children's book collection campaign for your classroom or donation to the nearest children's hospital.

9. Research making sand sculptures with your class.

10. Have your class pick the categories and write the questions for a classroom literature jeopardy game.

11. Discuss child-bearing laws of societies around the world. Then pose the problem that you live in a society that up until the age of twenty you must change parents every five years. How would this be accomplished? What would be the good and bad features of such a society?

12. Discuss TV shows, movies and stories where the pet talks and is very intelligent—Ben and Me, Rats of Nimh, Mr. Ed, etc.

13. Do scenario writing. What opening lines can we use when we want to discuss something serious or personal with someone?

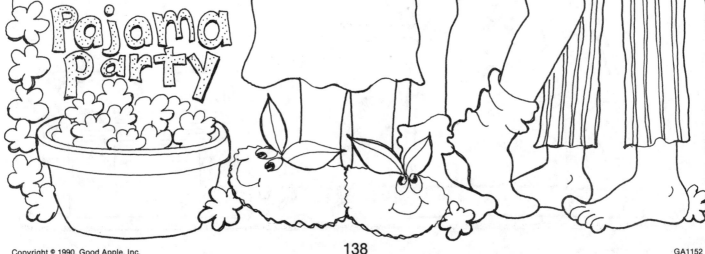

GA1152

Blubber

139

GA1152

 **Lead-Ins to Literature**

You are probably thinking that this is the story of the whaling industry. Where they are found, how they are hunted and what types of manufacturing surrounds the whaling industry will be detailed. Wrong guess! *Blubber* deals with children in everyday classroom situations. It does not show their best sides. It is amazing how insensitive children are to the feelings of other children. They tease and taunt about the silliest things. Often their lack of consideration for their classmates' feelings can do unrepairable harm. *Blubber* is such a story.

1. What are three of the most common things that children tease each other about?

    a. _____

    b. _____

    c. _____

2. What three things are you teased most often about?

    a. _____

    b. _____

    c. _____

3. What topics would you allow teasing to cover or would you eliminate teasing altogether?

    _____

4. How do you recommend a program be started to show people the effects of teasing? How would you start towards its elmination?

    _____

5. What effects have you seen in children who are constantly teased and picked on?

    _____

6. Have you ever gone out of your way to be friendly to someone whom you know that has few friends?

    _____

7. Do you make everyone welcome in your activities or do you play only with your special friends?

    _____

8. Can you devise three ways to make all kids feel good about themselves?

    _____

9. What was the best you ever felt in school? Explain.

    _____

10. In your estimation, who teases to excess more, boys or girls?

    _____

11. What do you think you will learn from this story?

    _____

Vexing Vocabulary

mammal
tangles
original
dolphin
approval
anxious
conversation
nineteen

cigarette
surprised
costumes
notice
faint
certain
gloss
unicef

stuffy
rude
sparkle
Maudie
groaned
chocolate
assembly
neighbor

Copy each vocabulary word to the left of the twenty-four lines below. Follow your teacher's directions as he/she instructs you to write a sentence of your own using each word. The author prefers that the student find the actual sentence in the story where each word appears. This is cumbersome at first, but necessary for realizing what relationship the vocabulary word has to the story. It also beats writing the word three times, then writing it in a sentence, then writing it in a paragraph for review. After completing this activity, turn to the back vocabulary section of the book, where you will find forty-eight creative ways to follow up this assignment. Pick two activities that are challenging to you and complete them on a separate sheet of paper.

1. _____
2. _____
3. _____
4. _____
5. _____
6. _____
7. _____
8. _____
9. _____
10. _____
11. _____
12. _____
13. _____
14. _____
15. _____
16. _____
17. _____
18. _____
19. _____
20. _____
21. _____
22. _____
23. _____
24. _____

GA1152

Sliding Letters I (Easy)
Drills for Skills
Activity and Gameboard Student Sheet

Sliding letters can be completed on this work sheet or by using the gameboard and cutout letters on the following pages. Each letter above the grid may slide downward one space or two spaces. If you slide each letter correctly, you will have an easy-to-recognize word on line one and an easy-to-recognize word on line two. There will be spaces between the letters on each line. Nevertheless, two words are clearly visible and the letters for each are in proper order. In this first challenge, each word has the same number of letters. Please be reminded that letters can only be moved downward, never left or right.

Example: **Starting Gate**

D	O	C	G	A	T

D	O		G		
		C		A	T

1.
R	T	U	I	G	P

2.
B	E	O	L	M	Y

3.
O	P	U	T	E	N

4.
F	A	O	L	R	L

5.
S	T	O	W	Y	L

6.
L	A	P	N	O	R	D	T

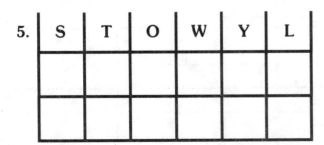

GA1152

Sliding Letters
Drills for Skills—Gameboard

Use this gameboard and the cutout letters to complete the problems presented on the student sheet. Place your letters in the starting gate above each grid. Move your letters downward to the positions that will solve each challenge. Design some challenges of your own that you can dictate to a classmate. The gameboard will work with games that use as many as twelve letters. If your task uses less than twelve letters, the last few starting gates will be empty.

A	B	C	D	E	F	G	H	I
J	K	L	M	N	O	P	Q	R
S	T	U	V	W	X	Y	Z	A
B	C	D	E	F	G	H	I	J
K	L	M	N	O	P	Q	R	S
T	U	V	W	X	Y	Z	A	A
E	E	I	I	O	O	U	S	T

Starting Gates

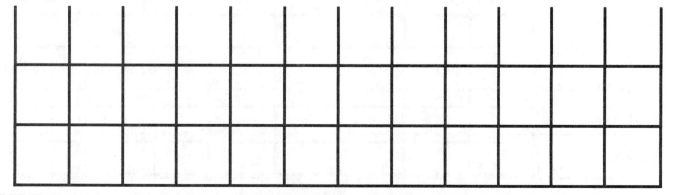

GA1152

Sliding Letters
Drills for Skills—Blank Gameboard

Your teacher will dictate letters that you will place from left to right in the starting gates below. The letters may be moved one or two spaces downward only. If you move the letters properly, you will have formed words of the same size on both rows A and B. There will be spaces between the letters, but the letters will be in word order.

Starting Gate

Row A

Row B

Starting Gate

Row A

Row B

Starting Gate

Row A

Row B

Starting Gate

Row A

Row B

Starting Gate

Row A

Row B

Starting Gate

Row A

Row B

GA1152

Research Suggestions

1. The whale is the largest living mammal. Can you draw and label the sizes from some of the smallest to largest?

2. *The Book of World Records* is mentioned in *Blubber*. Find three world records in each of the following areas: food consumption, travel, sports, bodily functions (say sleeping or eating), speeding and intelligence (man or animal).

3. What are the five most costly stamps? Sketch three of them. How much were they worth originally and how much are they worth now? Pick an area like flowers, sports or industry and investigate what U.S. stamps have been issued in these areas.

4. Your school probably has a parent/teacher organization. What were their last three projects? Interview the group's president and determine some future projects and directions the group will take.

5. Louis XIV of France was born with two front teeth. There must be something more notable to mention about him. After you write a brief synopsis of his life, pick the French king that you think is most memorable. Draw a mini sketch above your facts. The Garden of the Kings at Versailles is magnificent. Plan and draw your version of what the world's most exquisite garden should look like.

6. If you were leading a group discussion about feelings, what type of things would be your focus? How would you get the group or individual to share what is really bothering them? What solutions to the problems in *Blubber* can you recommend?

7. Create a trial that would put prejudice on the stand.

8. Design a "Hand in Hand We Can Make Our School Better" campaign.

9. Where is the nearest art and advertising firm in your area? Find out how they generate sign and billboard business. What kind of schooling do members of their staff have?

10. Compose a song or poem titled "Whispers Hurt."

11. Research the positive and negative side effects of three of the most used or well-known diets. Make a calorie and protein chart of these same three diets.

145

Additional Vexing Vocabulary Suggestions

One of the most important aspects of a good literature program is the development of vocabulary. Many children are great at reading words, but are lacking in word understanding and the ability to use the same words they have just read in other situations or in their own writing. The author feels strongly that these five stages of vocabulary development should be presented before formally teaching any book or reading selection.

1. Key Words/Introduction of Vocabulary

   Place each of the vocabulary words on the chalkboard. Make sure each student hears and practices the correct pronunciation of each word. Find out how many words are familiar to the students and concentrate on the new words. Have the children brainstorm from their own experience words that are similar in meaning and pronunciation to the words being introduced.

2. Dictation

   The most neglected part of a literature/vocabulary program is dictation. Students should be involved in some sort of dictation every day. This not only develops better vocabulary usage, but also develops writing and listening skills. You can dictate short sentences from reading selections or from any piece of the curricula that is used in your school. Combine your math and science terms in humorous sentences that also include your literature vocabulary. Spelling tests should include dictated sentences that are filled with the spelling vocabulary. Student assignments can include writing sentences that can be read to their peers during dictation sessions. Fifth through eighth graders should be given speed dictation, which again helps better listening, writing and note taking skills.

3. Comprehension Skills

   Comprehension is serious work. There aren't too many cute ideas to develop comprehension. Students must be taught context clues, reading for meaning, thesaurus usage, critical thinking and predicting the main idea/outcomes if they are to get the maximum enjoyment and education benefit from future literary selections.

4. Interpretive Reading

   The battle rages on over the benefits of silent and oral reading. If you agree with the use of either or both approaches then, of course, you would prepare the students before they read. The What Is Your Opinion section of this book tries to address this point. Interpretive reading and paragraph analysis is cumbersome because you need immediate feedback from the students after they have read a small section of work. This can be accomplished with a peer tutoring program or small group sessions where every student's point of view can be heard, discussed and modified.

5. Evaluation

   Consistent, meaningful and nonthreatening evaluations are essential in all literature programs. Read and test programs have greatly reduced the number of children excited about good literature. Simple ideas like tape-recording your thoughts for sharing, to dull book trials where you have to defend your book in court, to I wrote it but you won't believe me, have served the same purpose as the true and false test.

GA1152

Vexing Vocabulary Follow-Up Suggestions

1. Make a collage of cutout words that mean the same thing as ten words featured in your word list.

2. Make a giant connect-a-gram where the last letter in one of your words going across is the first letter of a new word going down.

3. Hide the letters in one of the words above in an illustration that describes the word.

4. Have an "I can spell it backwards" contest with one of your classmates. First one to get ten words correct is the winner. If you think spelling is tough forwards, this will be a real challenge.

5. Make a list of fifteen of the above words and next to it put fifteen words that have similar meanings. Exchange your list with a friend and draw lines connecting the correct matches. If you put a small strip of paper between your words so your neighbor can write on it, you can exchange your work with a number of different people.

6. Pick three words from the lists above that you feel comfortable using. Write three sentences using one word in each sentence. Under each vocabulary word write a new word that means the same thing. Score one point for each new word. Exchange your original sentence with a friend. See if he can develop more words than you that have the same meaning as your key word.

7. You are an architect of crossword puzzles. Design a crossword puzzle form and clues.

8. Make-believe you are a movie reviewer. Each word you select from above is a one-word title of a movie. Describe the movie but keep its relationship close to the original word.

9. Write an original poem using five of the words in the above list.

10. You are a word seller like in the marketplace of the Phantom tollbooth. Pick two words and give a short presentation as to the great benefits of buying these words from you.

11. Place one of these words in front of Mr. or Mrs. and describe your appearance and personality. An example would be Mr. Blah.

12. Make a poster pointing out that if there were only one word in the world, this would be your choice. Take a class survey of your classmates' word choices and their selection reasons.

13. Make up song titles using your vocabulary words in the titles. Use real or make-believe artists as the performers.

14. Give a famous wrestler one of the words as his title. Describe how he acquired this title. Illustrate his outfit's appearance in a wrestling scene.

15. Many people name their boats unique names. Incorporate one of the words in the word list in your boat title. Describe its significance in your life and the reason for naming the boat in such a way.

16. Pick five words that would be appropriate for a pet. Describe the pet and why this particular word choice is meaningful. Try to pick exotic pets or pets that aren't as common as a dog and a cat.

17. Write a radio commercial using five of the words from your list. Have a classmate time your presentation. It must be thirty seconds long.

GA1152

18. Can you think of five crazy, way out ideas to help people remember new words? An example would be a soup like alphabet soup. This soup has words floating in it. When you bite into each word, it gives you its meaning.

19. Design a beach towel and surfboard that features two of your vocabulary words. Explain why these words will attract people to your two products.

20. Design a poster attracting people to your town or city. Use five words from the word list as part of your promotion.

21. Make a humorous shield of one of the Knights of the Round Table who uses two of your vocabulary words in his motto.

22. Describe five leading characters from books other than Judy Blume's who could be described with Judy Blume vocabulary.

23. Onomatopoetic words are words that represent sounds. Pick five vocabulary words and see if you can write three onomatopoetic words that would relate to each one.

24. Pick five words that could be street names. Describe the happenings on each of their particular streets.

25. One of your vocabulary words is a hideous monster who is terrorizing the neighborhood. Draw a picture of the monster. Create a newspaper headline using the monster's vocabulary name. Write the story that goes with the headline and picture.

26. A couplet is a two-line poem. Both lines in a couplet rhyme. See if you can write three couplets that incorporate at least one of your vocabulary words on each line. The vocabulary word can be in the body of the line. An ultimate challenge is to see how many vocabulary words you can make part of the rhyme scheme.

27. A tercet is a three-line poem. It can have many rhyme schemes. For the purpose of this activity, each of the lines will rhyme. Have a contest with a classmate to see who can use the most vocabulary words in your tercet. Score one point if it is a vocabulary word in the heart of the line. Score two points if your vocabulary word rhymes at the end of a line.

28. A quatrain is a four-line stanza found in most poems. It also can have many rhyme schemes. For the purpose of this activity, the first and third lines will rhyme and so will the second and fourth lines. See how creatively you can use your vocabulary words in composing your own quatrain.

29. The Oregon Trail was known for the creative epitaphs that were found on tombstones along its route. They were supposed to serve as monuments to those buried there. See if you can compose an epitaph using three of your vocabulary words.

30. Create four lines for a rap song. Incorporate six of your vocabulary words in the song.

31. Write a want ad asking in a humorous fashion for someone to purchase your comic books, baseball cards or bicycle. Underline each vocabulary word that you insert in your ad.

32. Write ten *Jeopardy* questions and answers that highlight some of your vocabulary words.

33. Describe a performer—singer, movie star, TV star, dancer or animal star—using three of your vocabulary words.

GA1152

34. Write the *TV Guide* blurb that would accompany your favorite TV program. Write each vocabulary word that you use in capital letters.

35. Design a one-minute humorous public service announcement expounding on why these three vocabulary words of your choice should be excluded from the English language.

36. Write five sentences using the Pig Latin spelling and pronunciation of each of your vocabulary words.

37. Use a hanger and strips of paper to make a word mobile that will flutter your vocabulary words in the wind.

38. Design a shirt, skirt or pants that would have one of your vocabulary words as the brand name appearing on it.

39. Write an absence excuse using five of your vocabulary words. If it is really good, maybe your teacher will give you the day off.

41. Name five stars, planets, asteroids or constellations after your vocabulary words. Explain the way you bestowed that particular name on your celestial body.

42. Cut out pictures of five famous paintings. Change their titles to include some of your key words from the story.

43. Draw a racing car that has vocabulary words on it instead of advertisements of various motor oils and other products. You might want to do the same thing for the driver's jumpsuit, which usually looks like an advertising billboard.

44. Make a set of footprints. Each footprint will contain clues that will give your classmates a better understanding of their vocabulary words.

45. Make a clothesline of words. Each word will be incorporated into a descriptive picture. Under it will be a sentence that indicates you have a clear meaning of the way the word is used in the story. Most students write that the wound was bandaged. In reality the word was *wound*, like he wound the string around the tree. Be careful, please, with your word's context clues.

46. Talk your teacher into sponsoring a crazy hat and sneaker day. Each student designs a crazy hat and sneaker with props and five of their spelling words. The words must relate to the theme of the sneaker and hat. Classes participating can collect money that can be donated to the nearest children's hospital.

47. Putting on the hits, lip synchronize your favorite songs. Each song must contain your vocabulary words. Each word included in your song will be placed on cards. The card will be displayed like a video prop when you get to that section of the song.

48. Design a stained glass window scene that includes five of your vocabulary words.

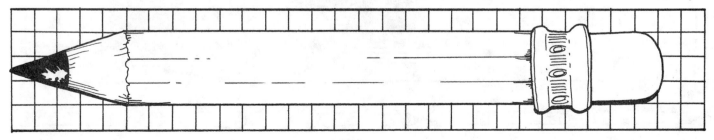

GA1152

Student-Generated Instruction

This portion of the book is designed to challenge you into taking a greater part in your own instruction. You can do this by designing classroom lessons using literature selections from Judy Blume or your favorite author. The lessons will be developed as if you were the classroom teacher. You have seen your teachers do it hundreds of times. You know what things worked and what ideas appeal to children in your age group. You have seen how stories are introduced. You have worked with fact and opinion. Short-term projects, ideas and illustrations and research should be, by this time in the program, some of your fortes. See if you can expand each book unit in this section with your own original, interesting and creative approaches to the way you feel literature should be taught. Recruit a five-member team. Assign each member a section of study for the book you are going to develop. I've started some Judy Blume books for you. You may want to follow the general outline we have been following throughout this book. If you don't, try striking out in an entirely new direction of your own. Ask your teacher to use your units with other classes. She may want to also save your ideas for next year's class. If your team's ideas are really good, put them in booklet form. Don't forget an attractive cover. If you have an exceptional art student in your group, have him make an additional booklet of just artwork that would support the book you developed. Fill out this information sheet. It will allow your classroom teacher to keep track of your team's assignments and progress.

The book we will develop is _____

The names of the students who will develop each section are

1. Lead-Ins to Literature _____

2. Just the Facts _____

3. What Is Your Opinion? _____

4. Ideas and Illustrations _____

5. Short-Term Projects _____

6. Research Suggestions _____

7. Teacher Suggestions _____

8. Drills for Skills _____

9. Vexing Vocabulary _____

10. Team Artist _____

GA1152

Student-Generated Instruction
Book Introduction Design Sheet

Review some of the cover pages that appear in this book. Design a cover for one of the books that your team has selected.

151

Starring Sally J. Freedman as Herself
Lead-Ins to Literature

It is 1947 and Sally's family is moving to Florida. The move will help Sally's brother, the Genius. His health isn't good following a bout with nephritis, a kidney infection. The move makes their family disjointed because her father has to stay in Elizabeth, New Jersey, because of his job. The new location and Sally's spy-and-World-War-II-not-being-over phobia take her through a wealth of new ideas, experiences and daydreams. Some nightmares also follow along, too. Maybe finding the boy of her dreams will make life in Florida more enjoyable. That is unless Mr. What-Is-His-Name gets her.

1. What kind of activities would children be in now that weren't possible in 1947?

_____

2. What types of technology and machinery do we use that wasn't available in 1947?

_____

3. Would you be happy moving from where you presently live, if the new location happened to be Florida?

_____

4. Radio programs and storytelling play an important role in this story. What type of topical stories would someone make up in 1947?

_____

5. Sally keeps on writing letters to Mr. Zavodsky, the man who she thinks is a spy. What type of actions by someone would convince you that he/she was a spy?

_____

6. Crime fighter and detective stories were big in 1947. What opening lines for a detective show could you write to attract people's attention to it week after week?

_____

7. Douglas invents a coconut retriever. How would someone operate such a device?

_____

8. Sally dreams of a play called "The White Shoulders" in which she happens to be starring. It is about World War II. What could she know about the war?

_____

9. Children always cleaned their plates of all food during the war. Why was this practiced in houses throughout the United States?

_____

10. Parents are always saying things in front of children. When you ask them what it means, they never tell you or just say, "Never mind." Why do you suppose they do this?

_____

GA1152

Starring Sally J. Freedman as Herself

Vexing Vocabulary

Andrea
Douglas
relieved
oscilloscope
romance
blotchy
infection
organdy

resemblance
whimpered
annoyed
abandoned
commotion
medicine
technician
balance

surrounded
squeezed
cushions
jealous
tinsel
recreation
pneumonia
impatient

Copy each vocabulary word to the left of the twenty-four lines below. Follow your teacher's directions as he/she instructs you to write a sentence of your own using each word. The author prefers that the student find the actual sentence in the story where each word appears. This is cumbersome at first, but necessary for realizing what relationship the vocabulary word has to the story. It also beats writing the word three times, then writing it in a sentence, then writing it in a paragraph for review. After completing this activity, turn to the back vocabulary section of the book where you will find forty-eight creative ways to follow up this assignment. Pick two activities that are challenging to you and complete them on a separate sheet of paper.

1. _____
2. _____
3. _____
4. _____
5. _____
6. _____
7. _____
8. _____
9. _____
10. _____
11. _____
12. _____
13. _____
14. _____
15. _____
16. _____
17. _____
18. _____
19. _____
20. _____
21. _____
22. _____
23. _____
24. _____

GA1152

Starring Sally J. Freedman as Herself
Two Letter Flyover
Drills for Skills

✴ Flip-flops are special word pairs. When you remove a letter from the beginning of the first word (CAR) and place it at the end of the remaining letters (AR), you create a new word (ARC). The letter seems to fly over the word. Two Letter Flyovers employ the same rule, only the first two letters fly to the end in the same order. These clues will help you to find the correct word pairs.

Clue 1	Clue 2	Answers
Example: Lately happenings/in the middle		**recent/centre**

1. Part of the head/unit of measure _____ _____
2. Health resort/Cleopatra's snake _____ _____
3. Burn meat/bottom of your foot _____ _____
4. One piece/give off light _____ _____
5. A drink/already eaten _____ _____
6. Opposite of *less*/comic, movie hero _____ _____
7. Picnic pest/color _____ _____
8. Opposite of *wild*/between or beyond prefix _____ _____
9. Alike/high plateau _____ _____
10. Snake-like fish/protected side _____ _____
11. A vegetable/jungle animal _____ _____
12. Small (Irish)/female sheep _____ _____
13. Likely/touch softly _____ _____
14. Boy's name/draw on glass _____ _____
15. Type of large tree/Alice's boss at the diner _____ _____

How many Two Letter Flyovers can you find? Create?

154

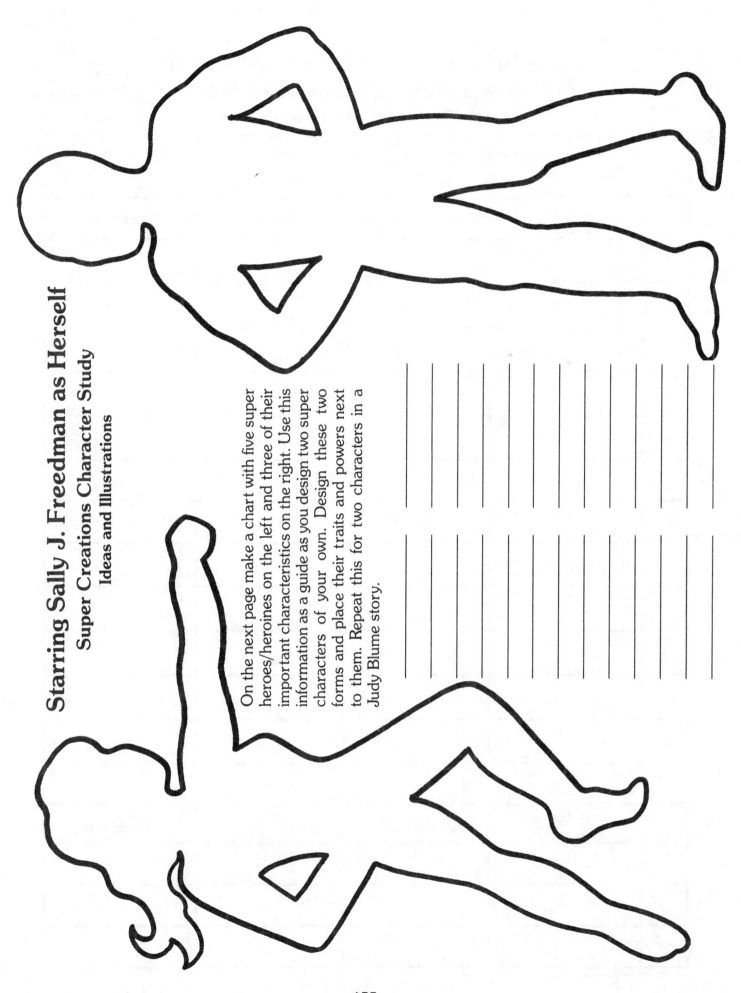

Starring Sally J. Freedman as Herself

Super Creations Character Study
Ideas and Illustrations

On the next page make a chart with five super heroes/heroines on the left and three of their important characteristics on the right. Use this information as a guide as you design two super characters of your own. Design these two forms and place their traits and powers next to them. Repeat this for two characters in a Judy Blume story.

GA1152

Starring Sally J. Freedman as Herself
Super Creations Character Study
Ideas and Illustrations/Short-Term Project

Place five super heroes/heroines in the left column. Record three of their characteristics in the columns that follow. Do the same for five cartoon characters and three Judy Blume characters.

	Super Characters	Features/Looks	Powers	Other
1.				
2.				
3.				
4.				
5.				

	Cartoon Characters	Features	Actions	Predicaments
1.				
2.				
3.				
4.				
5.				

	Judy Blume Characters	Features/Looks	Qualities/Traits	Problems
1.				
2.				
3.				

GA1152

The Pain and the Great One

City Building

Pulling Hair

Disgusting Things

Zooming Trucks

CAT

Like Best Contest

Playing Alone

GA1152

The Pain and the Great One
Vexing Vocabulary

kitchen
flakes
dressed
pokey
reason
ordinary
stuff
garbage

dessert
supposed
bathroom
powders
tucked
younger
tomorrow
fault

stupid
knocking
buildings
instead
especially
piano
drawer
dials

Copy each vocabulary word to the left of the twenty-four lines below. Follow your teacher's directions as he/she instructs you to write a sentence of your own using each word. The author prefers that the student find the actual sentence in the story where each word appears. This is cumbersome at first, but necessary for realizing what relationship the vocabulary word has to the story. It also beats writing the word three times, then writing it in a sentence, then writing it in a paragraph for review. After completing this activity, turn to the back vocabulary section of the book, where you will find forty-eight creative ways to follow up this assignment. Pick two activities that are challenging to you and complete them on a separate sheet of paper.

1. _____
2. _____
3. _____
4. _____
5. _____
6. _____
7. _____
8. _____
9. _____
10. _____
11. _____
12. _____
13. _____
14. _____
15. _____
16. _____
17. _____
18. _____
19. _____
20. _____
21. _____
22. _____
23. _____
24. _____

GA1158

The Pain and the Great One
Research Suggestions

1. What is sibling rivalry? What articles can you find on this subject in *Psychology Today, Parents Magazine, Reader's Digest, Redbook, Woman's Day* or any other over-the-counter magazine?

2. Cornflakes are everywhere, but what do we really know about them? What can you find out about research in the baby food industry? Make a mini scrapbook of articles relating to the food industry.

3. Make-believe that you are a Gerber salesperson. What products would you highlight in your catalog? Share your thoughts about new products that your company is developing.

4. The two lead characters fight concerning who mother likes the most. Can you make a scale or chart that will allow them to record specific information of Mom's likes and dislikes? Explain how this information will be evaluated to determine who mother likes the most. Why would any work of this sort be misleading?

5. Take three statements of the Pain's and three of the Great One's. Present the counter argument to each one.

6. List five things that a six-year-old will soon outgrow.

7. Research stupid songs. Make a list of the five best. Take one of the songs and make an advertising poster for it. Describe the type of humor being used. What is a parody?

8. What can you find out about the sleeping habits of cats, dogs and other animals? What is our internal time clock? What is the significance of the term *circadian rhythms*?

9. What percentage of your class takes piano lessons? Chart the lesson-taking choices of your classmates.

10. Visit your local furniture store. Find out what percentage of furniture sales is related to the purchase of baby furniture. Next to cribs, what is the most frequently purchased item?

11. What type of powders can be found in the bathroom? What are the price ranges of these powders? Can you recommend three different powders and the reason for your good rating of them?

12. Hats are illustrated throughout the book. Can you pick a country and research the evolution of hats in it? What kind of hats are worn in your area?

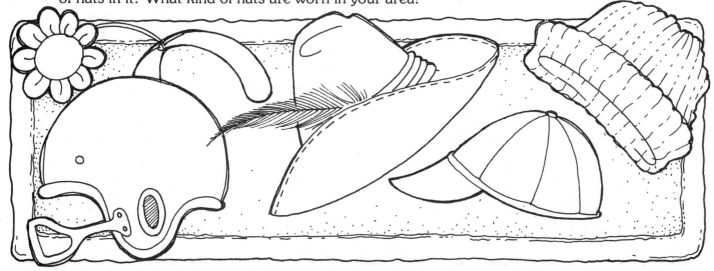

GA1152

The Pain and the Great One

Ideas and Illustrations

The Great One seems to enjoy wearing hats. You find her in everything from a cowboy hat to a football helmet. She also likes to decorate the hats that she wears. Below you will find a Sherlock Holmes hat, Australian cowboy hat, football helmet and baseball cap. Review the appearance of these hats in the story. Use color and design to give your impressions of the way they should look.

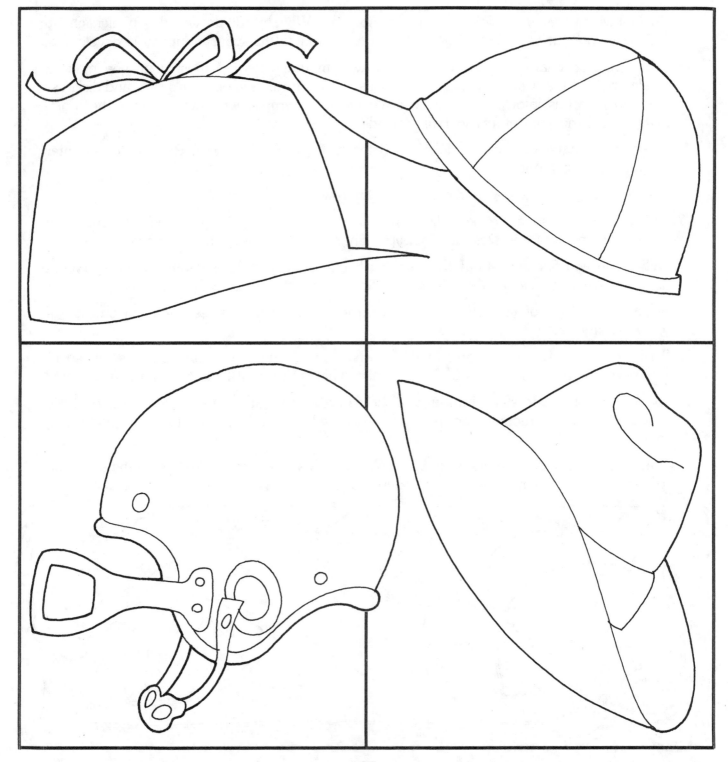

GA1152

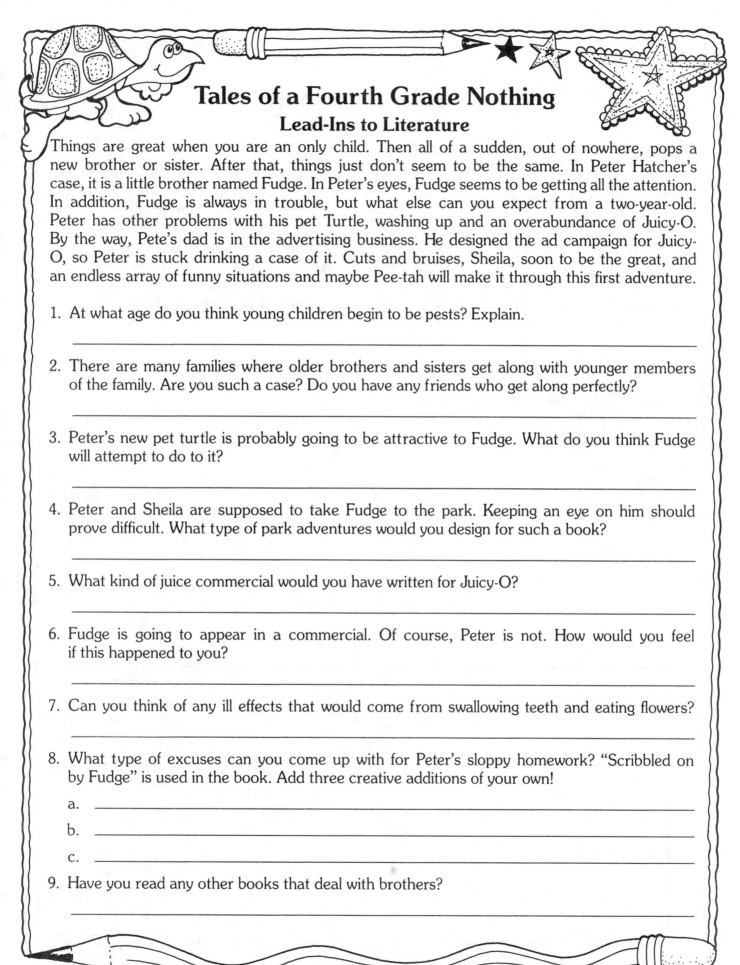

Tales of a Fourth Grade Nothing
Lead-Ins to Literature

Things are great when you are an only child. Then all of a sudden, out of nowhere, pops a new brother or sister. After that, things just don't seem to be the same. In Peter Hatcher's case, it is a little brother named Fudge. In Peter's eyes, Fudge seems to be getting all the attention. In addition, Fudge is always in trouble, but what else can you expect from a two-year-old. Peter has other problems with his pet Turtle, washing up and an overabundance of Juicy-O. By the way, Pete's dad is in the advertising business. He designed the ad campaign for Juicy-O, so Peter is stuck drinking a case of it. Cuts and bruises, Sheila, soon to be the great, and an endless array of funny situations and maybe Pee-tah will make it through this first adventure.

1. At what age do you think young children begin to be pests? Explain.

   _____

2. There are many families where older brothers and sisters get along with younger members of the family. Are you such a case? Do you have any friends who get along perfectly?

   _____

3. Peter's new pet turtle is probably going to be attractive to Fudge. What do you think Fudge will attempt to do to it?

   _____

4. Peter and Sheila are supposed to take Fudge to the park. Keeping an eye on him should prove difficult. What type of park adventures would you design for such a book?

   _____

5. What kind of juice commercial would you have written for Juicy-O?

   _____

6. Fudge is going to appear in a commercial. Of course, Peter is not. How would you feel if this happened to you?

   _____

7. Can you think of any ill effects that would come from swallowing teeth and eating flowers?

   _____

8. What type of excuses can you come up with for Peter's sloppy homework? "Scribbled on by Fudge" is used in the book. Add three creative additions of your own!

   a. _____

   b. _____

   c. _____

9. Have you read any other books that deal with brothers?

   _____

GA1152

Ideas and Illustrations Supplement
Bulletin Board

Dear teachers, students and bulletin board makers of America,

There are eight pages in this section. Each page contains two sections. The first section contains a hint for how you might want to decorate a teaching bulletin board in literature for the school year. The second part of each page is a bulletin board that has been started. It needs your input as to the direction that additional illustrations and writings should take. Please complete it with your original and humorous ideas. Two blank bulletin boards are provided below for students who would like to design a complete bulletin board on their own. Collect your classmates' ideas and put them in book form. Duplicate these books and send them to the various book companies that have similar literature in your school. Your class might get lucky and begin a whole new career in writing children's books.

January's Ideas, etc.

Bulletin Board Idea for September

Starting Off with Great Books

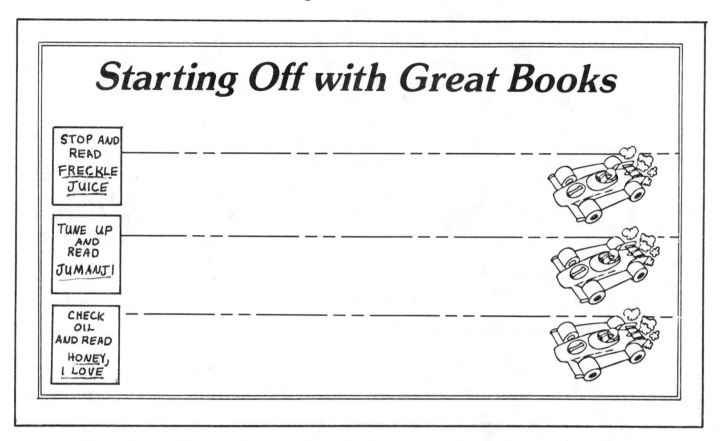

Starting Off with Great Books

STOP AND READ *FRECKLE JUICE*

TUNE UP AND READ *JUMANJI*

CHECK OIL AND READ *HONEY, I LOVE*

Student-Developed Bulletin Board for September

I Go Crazy over Books

I Go Crazy over Books

GO

PIT CREW

GA1152

Bulletin Board Idea for October

Good Books Scare Us

Student-Developed Bulletin Board for October

Classic Scary Books

Classic Scary Books

GA1152

Bulletin Board Idea for November

Score a Touchdown with These Judy Blume Classics

Student-Developed Bulletin Board for November

Turkeys Don't Read

GA1152

Bulletin Board Idea for December

Judy Blume Books Are a Snowman's Dream

Judy Blume Books Are a Snowman's Dream

Student-Developed Bulletin Board for December

Books Are Mind-Boggling Presents

Books Are Mind-Boggling Presents

Bulletin Board Idea for January

Tyrannosaurus Wrecks but Loves Judy Blume Books

Student-Developed Bulletin Board for January

Be a Literature Winner

GA1152

Bulletin Board Idea for February

Books Are Heartwarming

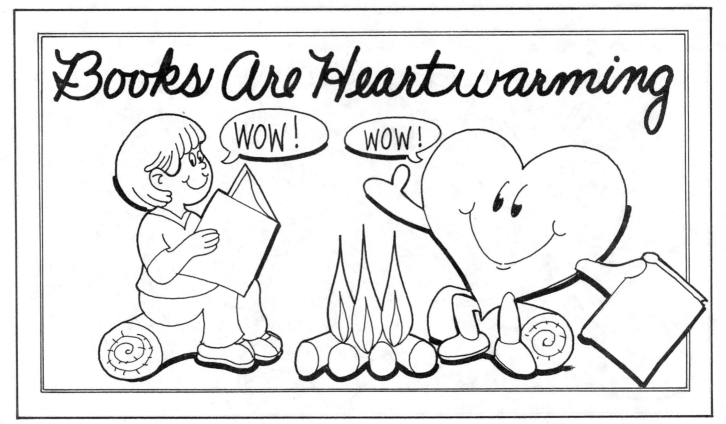

Student-Developed Bulletin Board for February

Do Not Foget These Valentine Love Stories and Poems

Do Not Forget These Valentine Love Stories and Poems

Bulletin Board Idea for March

Fishing for Good Books

Student-Developed Bulletin Board for March

Either Fly a Kite or Read a Good Book

GA1152

Bulletin Board Idea for April

We Are Having Fun Blume-ing

We Are Having Fun Blume-ing

Tiger Eyes

BLUBBER

SUPERFUDGE

Student-Developed Bulletin Board for April

Bell-Ringing Books for Spring

Bell-Ringing Books for Spring

On your own, try to create two bulletin boards for May, June, July and August.

Answer Key

Children's Literature Quotient, pages 4-5

A. 1. G, Katherine Paterson
2. K, Bernard Waber
3. I, Madeleine L'Engle
4. H, Eloise Greenfield
5. E, Judy Blume
6. C, Judith Viorst
7. J, Eleanor Coerr
8. A, Maurice Sendak
9. D, Beverly Cleary
10. B, Peter Mayle
11. F, Robert Kraus

B. 1. Where the Sidewalk Ends
A Light in the Attic
2. Alice in Wonderland
Through the Looking Glass
3. Weird Tales
The Gold Bug and Other Tales of Mystery
4. Stuart Little
Charlotte's Web
5. The Prince and the Pauper
The Adventures of Tom Sawyer
6. The Pain and the Great One
Freckle Juice
7. Rose, Where Did You Get That Red?
Teaching Great Poetry to Children
The Duplications
8. Answers will vary.
9. Answers will vary.
10. Answers will vary.

C. Newbery: Katherine Paterson, Bridge to Terabithia, 1977
Caldecott: Ezra Jack Keats, The Snowy Day, 1963

D. 1. A rhymed nonsense poem of five lines; rhyme scheme aabba
2. A story that includes the use of pictures
3. Words that have two meanings. Lewis Carroll used these.
4. "Why" stories
5. Repeated initial sound; a tongue twister using consonants
6. Repeated medial sound; a tongue twister with vowel sounds
7. Carrying on in couplet meters in a sentence beyond the end of a couplet into the next
8. The formation of words by imitating sounds, for example, fizz
9. A comparison of two unlike things using *like* or *as*, for example: Her face was as red as a beet.
10. Japanese form of poetry, usually about nature; 3 lines with a 5-syllable, 7-syllable, 5-syllable pattern, used to be only written by men

Just the Facts, page 39

1. 11, 8
2. 6th, 5th
3. Tokyo
4. Detroit
5. Clarice Landon
6. Answers will vary.
7. She was supposed to put in the dog's water.
8. Plays bridge
9. Mr. Berger, Miss Landon
10. They weren't wild about Clarice or her mom.

Vexing Vocabulary I, page 50

1. allergic
2. eighty degrees
3. headless horseman
4. newsdate
5. remarkable

Just the Facts, page 52

1. 10
2. Disneyland
3. English professor
4. Dogs, swimming, dark, spiders, thunder
5. New York
6. Washington Irving
7. Pottery
8. The title of Sheila's first story
9. As big as apples
10. Tell-the-truth book about friend's face, hair and body
11. They don't look anything alike—shy, quiet.
12. Swim across pool, tread water for two minutes

Buy or Sell, page 58

1. bunny, 2/5
2. swell, 1/5
3. busy, 1/4
4. buoy, 1/4
5. shell, 1/5
6. bully, 2/5
7. smell, 1/5
8. busy, 1/4
9. beauty, 3/6
10. shellac, 3/7
11. beauty, 3/6
12. stellar, 3/7

Just the Facts—True and False page 65

1. false, Jersey Journal
2. false, cancer removal of larynx
3. false, grandma
4. true
5. false, worry/problems
6. true
7. false, five
8. true
9. false, phone prank name
10. true

GA1152

Compound Word Intersections, page 71

1. breakdown = 88, oxcart = 90
2. overcoat= 18, bowtie = 91
3. seesaw = 50, boyhood = 35
4. anybody = 28, income = 36
5. everyone = 56, sunburn = 24
6. housefly = 10, breadbox = 32
7. printout = 56, teaspoon = 10
8. bookcase = 66, bathroom = 15
9. ice cream = 60, place mat= 40
10. body cast = 42, headrest = 24
11. myself = 35, playpen = 70

One, Two, Three, page 95

A. 2, B. 2, C. 3, D. 1, E. 2, F. 1, G. 2, H. 2, I. 1, J. 2, K. 1, L. 2 M. 2, N. 2, O. l, P. 1 der woman, Q. 1, R. 2

Just the Facts, page 99

1. four times in the chest
2. 7
3. a knife
4. first-day-in-high-school illness
5. anxiety
6. Project Y
7. high altitude
8. hiking boots
9. Wolf's dad
10. California
11. religious scientists . . . guilt and fear
12. Tiger
13. when the lizards run
14. Driver's Ed.
15. a bear
16. the nerd
17. *Oklahoma*
18. heart-shaped cookies
19. lettuce
20. Davey's T-shirt present from Ned

Vexing Vocabulary, page 111

1. two
2. middle
3. bow
4. room
5. pinched
6. Freddy
7. good luck
8. easy
9. extra hard
10. dreams

Literature Squares, pages 126-127

```
A. H E A V E N          E. H A D E S
   E         E             E       C
   R         S             L       O
   M         T             E       T
   E         L             N U R I T
   S T A B L E

B. A M E L I A          F. D A V I D
   R       R               W       R
   G       T               A       I
   Y       I               R       V
   L       S               F A B L E
   E R N E S T

C.                      G.
   T W A I N               P I P P I
   I     O                 E       R
   G     B                 D       E
   E     L                 R       N
   R U B L E               O L I V E

D. H E A R T S
   O       T
   T       E
   R       V
   O       E
   D R A G O N
```

Sliding Letters I, page 142

1. TUG RIP, TIP RUG
2. BOY ELM
3. OUT PEN
4. FOR ALL
5. STY OWL
6. LAND PORT

Drills for Skills, page 154

1. chin, inch
2. spa, asp
3. char, arch
4. item, emit
5. tea, ate
6. more, Remo
7. ant, tan
8. tame, meta
9. same, mesa
10. eel, lee
11. pea, ape
12. wee, ewe
13. apt, tap
14. Chet, etch
15. elm, Mel

GA1152